PRAISE FOR
THE *Voices of the 21st Century* BOOKS

The Women Speakers Association presents this valuable and inspiring collection of women from around the world who have made a difference and share their messages to aid other women in empowering themselves.

These are stories of women in all types of avenues who have gained not only stature, but also the respect of their peers, and now with this publication, the public! Each story is accompanied by a photograph of the speaker and a brief bio. The result is a collection of personal, conversational stories by a myriad of women from all manner of cultures and businesses, stories that inspire others to achieve a meaningful life. These women prove that women now assume the importance they have earned and deserve! Very impressive and highly recommended.

—Grady Harp, Hall of Fame Top 100 Reviewer

I've been amazed and inspired by this collective work. Every author has a personal experience and ideas to share to help each of us make a positive difference in our life. I found some stories reassuring, and others inspiring. These women offer support and guidance, so this is a fabulous resource for personal development and motivation for success.

—T-J Hughes

Inspiring, uplifting, life-affirming—this gem of a book contains fifty personal stories of extraordinary beauty from ordinary women who have shared their experiences. Uplifting and inspiring, each one takes only a few minutes to read, but will stay with you.

—Bridget Finklaire

While there are plenty of powerful and influential women to choose from in the history books, some people may be hard-pressed to point to role models in today's world. Even regular women from every walk of life can mentor and be a role model for us. This book is a collection of stories taken from these strong, smart, and resourceful women that showcase the obstacles they have overcome, how they learned from these situations, and how they ended up successful in the end. There is a lot to unpack—stories range from overcoming cancer to building a business and showing kindness in the face of adversity.

Empowering and well written, it is easy to be inspired by the stories. Different chapters will speak to different people, and I'm sure everyone can find a favorite within these pages. Each lady who has a story in here is pictured and we are given a way of finding more out about them. This is nice in the instance that one or more in particular inspires you in your life.

—*J. Armstrong*

As I read *Voices of the 21st Century*, I felt I stood in the midst of greatness. Most of these women take a burden, trial, or heartache and convey the wisdom and lessons they learned through it. Their goal is to encourage others and ignite a passion to rise above their suffering. Each of these women has reached a point in their life where they became a champion over their pain—and you can too.

I found *Voices of the 21st Century* to be an incredible collection of stories that stir my admiration to these women who have faced some horrible events in their lives, then turn around and say, "I survived and you can also."

When you finish reading this book, you will feel amazed, but also inspired to use your own story to touch others.

—*JoJo Maxson*

This book consists of a group of short essays designed to help women of any age as they make their way through the twists and turns that constitute daily life. Whatever your emotional challenge is, someone in this book has been there. It could be dealing with the death of a spouse, attempting to survive, let alone thrive, in a male-dominated field like construction, being in an emotional rut, or the aftermath of being shot by an AK-47. They show how they came out the other side, with the help of spirituality, a new mindset, or simply not giving up.

The essays are short—just a couple of pages each. This book can easily be read while waiting at the doctor's office, or at the grocery store. This book can be picked up and read starting on any page. Very much recommended!

—*Paul Lappen*

This compilation of essays written by women is a magnificent display of the resilience and strength of the 21st century woman in all her diversity. Through the sharing of personal struggles and challenges they have faced, readers will find a sense of comradery with each of the profiles in this book. Stories of loss, disappointment, illness, and unimaginable adversity, any of which would be reason enough to fall into despair, are related with the purpose of reaching and encouraging those who may be going through similar life experiences.

It is a book of triumph, of finding purpose in the face of great anguish and, most important, in giving back. Every story has something to teach and leaves one with an inspired view of what is possible. *Voices of the 21st Century* will leave you questioning your own purpose in life, but also will give you plenty of inspiration to seek that purpose. One of the best books about female empowerment I have read! It should be on the reading list of every woman and man who wishes to find inspiration within the lives of real women who have come through the storm and found strength on the other side. This wonderful group of essays and stories would make a wonderful gift for older teenage girls or graduates embarking upon the new world of college or starting a career.

—*Kat Kennedy*

Thank you for this book! This book was a very easy read for me, but it packed so much knowlege and wisdom. There is power in our words and power when we as women can collaborate. The principles taught in this book are simple yet effective. Anyone who reads this book will be become better equipped to accelerate spiritually, personally, emotionally, physically and purposefully. Thanks again!

—*Tschanna Taylor*

A beautiful collection of inspiring women! We are living in an awakening era for women, no doubt about it. From the #MeToo and #TimeIsUp movements, to protests to give a woman the right to choose over her body, women are fighting like never before for equality, recognition, and respect. Although the fight is necessary, sometimes the arguments and examples get repetitive; *Voices of the 21st Century* is a breath of fresh air. I liked how the stories are heart-moving, real, concise, and meaningful. I loved this book.

—*Lorenza Seldner*

I expected *Voices* to be a book about the "everyone can do it, you just need to have the determination" sort of thing. But it wasn't, and that's the best part. It is just a book about inner strength, determination, grit, and courage. That's it, and that's what makes it so empowering and inspiring.

This book hits right at the heart of a very pertinent issue today—women empowerment. With all the arguments for and against giving women equal status as men, and so many "patriarchal" and male-dominated customs and traditions being challenged on a global scale, this book comes forward as a strong point in favor of. It busts some old notions and beliefs and challenges archaic thinking. It is a collection of stories from strong women who made some very hard decisions and faced a lot of adversity, emerging victorious in one way or another in the end. It was a truly powerful read.

—*Priyanka Athavale*

To see the previous books in the *Voices of the 21st Century* series, *Women Who Influence, Inspire, and Make a Difference* and *Bold, Brave, and Brilliant Women Who Make a Difference,* visit https://voicesofthe21stcentury.com/buynow.

VOICES OF THE 21ST CENTURY

*Powerful, Passionate Women
Who Make a Difference*

GAIL WATSON

PUBLISHING

Published by WSA Publishing
301 E 57th Street, 4th fl New York, NY 10022
Copyright © 2020 by Women Speakers Association

Manufactured in the United States of America, or in the United Kingdom when distributed elsewhere.

Watson, Gail
Voices of the 21st Century: Powerful, Passionate Women Who Make a Difference

LCCN: 2020901679
ISBN: 978-1-951943-05-9
eBook: 978-1-951943-06-6

Cover design: Natasha Clawson
Copyediting: Claudia Volkman
Proofreading: Deb Coman
Interior design: Claudia Volkman

www.womenspeakersassociation.com

DEDICATION

We dedicate this book to each and every woman around the globe.
You all have a message. Your courage, kindness, and caring make a
difference. We see you and are grateful.

CONTENTS

FOREWORD

Melanie Benson

A passion-fueled woman with a commitment to make a difference is an unstoppable force for good on this planet.

And yet many women will keep that message locked up in their hearts, with maybe a whisper shared to a friend over lunch. A glimmer of passion ignited as she sends her last child off to college, only to simmer as she immerses herself back into daily life. A twinge of possibility as she watches Oprah's *Super Soul Sunday* that dies down as she heads back to her job. Too many women push down that passion and later wonder "What if . . ."

What if I had been brave enough to share my message in a bigger way?

What if I had been bold enough to risk it all to make a bigger difference?

What if I had courageously faced my inner critic and stepped into the spotlight?

What if I had inspired others—even one other person— to achieve their dreams too?

What if I allowed myself to shine bright enough to transform the lives of those I was meant to serve?

What if you knew that there is a community of people who need what you have in your heart and your mind in order to be fulfilled, happy, and healthy? Would you step up and get that message out in a bigger way?

When you feel that stirring in your heart, that call to step up and share your experience with others, that deep pull to awaken greatness in the hearts and minds of the world, then it's time to shine.

The world you are meant to serve is waiting for you.

I've been mentoring thought leaders, change makers, and

expert-entrepreneurs for twenty years now. I've had the privilege to hold space for many women on a mission and watch them conquer their mental gremlins to make a major impact on the world. A woman on a mission can be one of the most powerful forces on the planet. On her own, with her passion stoked and clear steps mapped out, she can be a force to be reckoned with. However, a woman surrounded by other powerful, passionate women grows wings that give her the strength to soar over obstacles and unforeseen roadblocks. A passion-fueled woman in a collaborative community is unstoppable.

In this book, you'll discover the message of women who have channeled their passion into a mission to make a difference. By joining forces with the other women of Women Speakers Association on the pages of *Voices of the 21st Century*, these messengers will grow wings that expand their reach beyond their wildest dreams.

This is the power of collaboration.

Women surrounded by other powerful women tap into the momentum of the collective. Think of it like the Tour de France. There are moments when a rider takes the lead in the race, but most riders can't stay in the lead without getting tired. The leader is setting the pace, but also has the wind working against them. Most of the riders take turns drafting the pace set by the lead racer. By sharing the lead/draft momentum, they stay in the race and outpace the performance they could achieve on their own.

As messengers in a collaborative community, we can "draft" momentum when we need it most. The days when we stop believing in our dream. When the fears are high, and the evidence of impact is low. When confidence has been crushed, and your self-doubt is trying to talk you into getting a "safe" job. This is when we need to tap into the momentum of other powerful women who believe in you and your mission.

As a part of the Executive Leadership Team and a founding member of Women Speakers Association for ten years, I have had the privilege of witnessing women from all over the world shatter their limits in the Own Your Bold® Influence program so they can make a difference in the world. I see firsthand how collaboration in community can provide the perspective and resources required to play a bigger game—even when you don't know if you can pull it off.

You can step into your greatness alone. But power is amplified when passion-driven women come together on a mission.

I hope that, as you read each word on these pages, you feel the collective power emerging and say YES to your dream. The world you are meant to serve needs your message.

Melanie Benson, *host of Own Your Bold®* *Challenge, is a Success Amplifier. She hosts the* Amplify Your Success Podcast, *is author of* Rewired for Wealth, *co-author of Entrepreneur.com's* Start Up Guide to Starting an Information Marketing Business, *and her success tips are featured in* Bloomberg Business Week, Woman's Day, *and* Parenting Magazine.

www.melaniebenson.com

Your Unique Message

Gail Watson

*It doesn't matter . . . no one will care. . . who are you to give that advice? . . .
no one wants to listen . . . you're not the expert . . . you don't bring value . . .*

These are the haunting voices that have run through my mind many
times for many years, and I know I'm not alone because I hear similar
things on a daily basis from women from all around the world in our
conversations.

One of the most painful points in a conversation is when someone
associates themselves with not bringing any value.

What I have come to learn and truly believe is that each one of us has
been gifted with a unique message. A message that that only we can share.

Please imagine your message sitting in the middle of your soul. Picture it
wrapped beautifully with your favorite color ribbon tied in a bow around it.
This gift is for you to give. Now imagine the receiver of your precious gift
opening it. As they do, it bursts open, a strong beam of light is released, and
it brightens up the entire room. You can feel the warmth from the light and
see flecks of glitter shimmering through it, almost like fairy dust. Your receiver
absorbs the warmth of the light and feels its power. The message you gave them
was just what they needed. Perhaps it was hope, inspiration, guidance, strength,
reassurance, a much-needed laugh, or letting them know they are not alone.

I believe that our messages find the right people, at the right time, to
make the right difference in their lives. By understanding and accepting
that your gifted message is meant to make a difference in the lives of others,
it then becomes your responsibility to share it—because if you don't, it
loses its power, and YOU can't do what you were intended to do.

What about those voices in your head that have convinced you that you
are not worthy or not good enough or that your message doesn't matter?
I'm here to tell you that you are worthy, you are good enough, and your

message definitely matters. Messages that have the power to influence our thoughts, to challenge the status quo, to inspire us to do better, to believe in ourselves, and to let us know we are not in this alone—these messages give us hope and cause for celebration.

If you are feeling stuck and you want to get past your limiting beliefs, here are some easy steps to get you ready to share your message:

1. "You are the sum of the five people you hang around with the most." We've all heard this old saying, and it's true. Our environment and who we surround ourselves with are critical to supporting our change and growth. Think about the type of person that you are. Are you entrepreneurial? Do you like to be around positive people? Do you like to be around driven people? Do you like connecting with others? Do you like learning? Do you believe you have a message? If you are surrounding yourself with others that don't inspire you or empower you or are active role models for you, its OK to limit the amount of time you spend with them. Just like a good spring cleaning rids your home of items that don't serve you anymore, the same is true with people in your life. You will be surprised at how fast you'll see improvement in yourself, and you'll realize it's quite easy to do this.

2. What we put into our mind first thing is our fuel for the day. Our mind doesn't know the difference between what's real and what's not—and this is a good thing because it means we can consciously control it. Since I'm not one who can sit and meditate, I've created my own way of meditation using social media; perhaps this will work for you too. I went through all the accounts that I follow on Instagram and deleted any negative ones (yes, including some friends). I searched out accounts that shared positive affirmations, positive guidance, and empowered kindness. Each morning, when I am having my coffee, I scroll my Instagram feed and take in quick positive quotes, inspiring messages, and colorful pictures that keep it simple. All these messages make me feel good, and it's a great way to start the day! Quite often during a conversation with someone in the Women Speakers Association community, I will share a quote that I had read that morning. This is how you can use social media as a tool to work for you and with you.

3. Learn the 20-20-20 Rule. My mentor, Anne-Marie, gave me the best advice years ago when I asked her to share her secret in life for staying so balanced. She taught me that we should always have someone in our life who is twenty years older and someone who is twenty years younger. The older one will offer us guidance, wisdom, experience, help us keep life in perspective, and give us permission to screw up and know it's not the end of the world. The younger one will excite us, keep our thinking fresh, challenge our thoughts, teach us some different ways of doing things, help us to learn patience, and show us that our words are very important to them. Having someone twenty-plus and twenty-below on either side of you will provide you with balance.

Be conscious and selective with your daily environment. Having the right people around you and receiving the right information will be the easiest way for you to overcome negative self-talk and create success within yourself. If you don't know where to start, I invite you to join a like-minded community of messengers. This is why Women Speakers Association was created. It's online, and it's easy to engage and surround yourself with others who are like you.

Gail Watson is president and founder of Women Speakers Association (WSA), the go-to place for innovative leaders, change-agents, and women with a message to connect, collaborate, and grow their visibility worldwide in order to fulfill their mission. As the first-ever global community for women speakers, WSA provides a platform for women to get seen, booked, and paid AND be part of a growing network reaching women in 120 countries.

www.womenspeakersassociation.com

TUMBLE, TUMBLE, POLISH, AND SHINE

Desiree Aragon

Every year I host an annual women's conference. This started five years ago with a gentle longing to connect with my friends and colleagues. The goal? To begin the new year in a joy-filled and optimistic way. The first event was done retreat-style with an overnight stay. We shared three meals together and laughed and cried. Six of my closest friends attended and we chose the theme of easing into the new year.

Five years later we had more than eighty women in attendance. The format evolved into a half-day luncheon. We came together this year with the theme of standing strong. Our talented women speakers shared stories of owning our joy, finding our grit, and leveraging strategic partnerships. This all made me curious.

What does it mean to stand strong as a woman in this modern world?

Three years ago, my whole world was turned upside down, with the end of my marriage and changes in residence and work life all happening at the same time. Waves of strong emotions, missed opportunities, and disappointments hit repeatedly and just kept tumbling over and over again. I had worked through my twenties and found professional success as a corporate executive. I was leading our family, growing two beautiful humans—when suddenly all of it just looked different. It wasn't that it no longer mattered; it was that it mattered so much that something had to change.

Some people commented that it seemed like an identity crisis. My ex-husband said with exasperation, "I don't even know who you are anymore." Yet I knew who I was. I felt more certain than ever that I KNEW myself. I am a spiritual seeker eager to practice the behaviors that light the way for us all to live joyful, peaceful lives. I am a passionate thought leader put on this earth to celebrate talented women doing what they do best.

So how could feeling so certain of my personal truth create a situation where everything in my life could just fall apart?

Ahh. That was it. It wasn't my husband's truth or my children's truth or my parents' truth. It was *my* truth. Up to that point, I had so capably been helping everyone else live in their truth that I was losing mine. I became what others needed and wanted. I followed all the paving stones up the corporate ladder and into the marriage with two kids, two dogs, and a lovely four-bedroom family home.

The "identity crisis" did not come from not knowing my truth; it came from not LIVING my truth.

My truth was not in the neighborhood where everyone looked and talked alike. My truth was not in the school where my children struggled to fit in because they were different in personality and learning styles. My truth was not at the country club where my golf-loving husband felt most at home. My truth is in spiritual exploration and deep philosophical conversations. My truth is in the mess, the uncertainty, and the discoveries. My truth is in a diversity of opinions, lifestyles, and self-expression.

What started as a simple conversation about living true to oneself tumbled into a giant mess of a divorce, financial reversals, and long nights of questioning and doubting myself. However, I was determined not to give up on who I knew myself to be. The person who I had found in my twenties had become stuffed behind an image of a woman who had her shit together. A shell.

It turns out that living in my truth hasn't been pretty. As a matter of fact, it wasn't pretty at all. It involved counseling, parenting classes, yoga, meditation, and mental health treatment. It was gritty and messy and sometimes ugly. Like rocks being placed into a tumbler, everything was being refined. The good news is, though, that after rocks repeatedly tumble in a rock tumbler, they go through a cleansing process with water and rock polish. Afterward the rocks are transformed into brightly polished stones ready to shine.

This journey of living in my truth started out rough and impolite, filled with anger and sorrow. It evolved, less rough but still a bit bristly and needing time and attention to continue to soften the hard edges. Slowly life began to be purified with moments of clarity and forgiveness.

Had you asked me this question fifteen years ago, I might have said that standing strong means maintaining your composure through difficult challenges. This most recent journey, however, has shown me that sometimes the outer layer just isn't deep enough. It may have the appearance of strength and blend into its environment, but its real beauty has yet to be discovered. I've learned that creating an appearance of having one's shit together is not actually the same as having it together.

So, what *does* it mean to stand strong as a woman in this modern world? For me, standing strong as a woman in this modern world means:

- Pressing on in the gentlest of ways when the going gets tough
- Saying no to anything that does not feel true and right
- Saying yes only to the things that align 100 percent
- Keeping an open heart even when it has been shattered into bits
- Celebrating successes, all of them, small and big

Standing strong in my truth no matter what is the cleansing step of my journey. It's discovering resiliency as I tumble and fall and purifying my thoughts and actions to match the person I know myself to be. And when it's time to polish this transformed version of myself, I am thrilled to say that I will not only be sparkling on the outside, but finally the shine will be coming from within.

Desiree Aragon is a talent champion. She inspires women to discover what they do best and to maximize potential when it matters most. She is certified to train and facilitate top-rated leadership programs, and she assists her clients to deliver difficult messages and influence with the power of persuasion.

www.desireearagon.com

I Hear an Elephant Call My Name

Carol Ann Joy Arnim

I am chatting outside a Whitehorse, Yukon, grocery with a woman I just met and the words that spontaneously erupt from me catch me by surprise. "One day soon I am going to go work with an elephant in Thailand." As I walk away, I ponder, *Wow, where did that come from?* Yet I know the words will indeed ring true, since that is how my life magically unfolds.

After eight months in high Arctic Canada, I am called back to dog sit in Whitehorse. My friend Chris and I somehow get talking about elephants, and that line I spoke months ago, again comes forth. The two of us are now excitedly discussing our love of the largest land mammal on the planet. "You know, my son knows a woman who volunteered at an elephant camp in Thailand."

My free-spirited manner takes over. Within less than forty-eight hours, I am signed up to go work with my own elephant north of Bangkok. Shortly after my dog sitting job is done, I am on my way.

As my taxi enters this working elephant camp, my home for the next ten days, I am indeed shocked at the sight before me. There are many elephants, all confined on short chains.

My girl, Jumpee, constantly sways to and fro when tied in her corral. By the end of my time with her, we have formed a bond. The night of my departure, I lay in tears. Her presence comforts me, thanking me for coming. "I wish I could bust you out of there, Jumpee."

"Thank you for such kind words spoken from your compassionate heart; however, I could not leave everyone else behind. It was my voice whom guided you here. We shall see each other again."

About a month later, thanks to Mr. Google, I am in eastern Cambodia about to experience the other end of the spectrum of elephant life. I am on a long hike with a guide and a couple other people to go find three elephants who are roaming free. My first sight of the threesome makes my heart sing with unbelievable relief and joy. Their color takes me by surprise because it looks like their bodies have all been dipped in a huge coating of chocolate. They have been in the nearby creek having the grandest time rubbing themselves in the mud. Their caretakers, the *mahouts*, are nearby. These fortunate creatures do whatever they want all day, and at night they are confined on a very long chain to prevent them from ravaging nearby plantations.

Humans have been riding elephants for countless years, taking them into battle, and working with them in the logging industry and tourism. Extensive abuse has resulted. A very few ethical sanctuaries where elephants are not allowed to be ridden now exist. The issue to ride versus not ride is controversial. Elephants provide a source of income to many. Countless people travel to southeast Asia to fulfill their wishes of riding an elephant.

A few weeks ago, I was one of those people. Yet I believe that is why my Jumpee was the elephant who whispered to me in my daydreams, waiting for the divine timing to allow me to manifest my arrival to her home. I needed to experience firsthand how she spent her days and nights. Humanity is slowly awakening to a more evolved and respectful treatment of animals. Considering my love for animals, I did feel ashamed to have played a part in her captive lifestyle. Every time I saw the mahout place the chains back on her, it filled me with guilt and sorrow.

Yet it is thanks to this beautiful soul gracing the body of Jumpee that I went on to further travels to Cambodia, Vietnam, and Laos. A couple days after my acceptance to volunteer at the Thai elephant camp, I applied as a volunteer in both Saigon and Hanoi, Vietnam. Ten challenging, incredible life-changing weeks in Vietnam working with children and war veterans impacted by Agent Orange leave me forever changed. A former life as an American flyer dumping Agent Orange spoke to me, asking me to go right a wrong.

So, it is with the highest reverence and gratitude to Jumpee for guiding me to successfully fulfill my mission of compassion to southeast Asia that spurs me on to help her and other elephants connected to the tourism industry. For anyone reading this story who might be considering how to spend time with elephants, I encourage you to seek out the ethical elephant sanctuaries where those elephants blessed to roam free can be experienced. An elephant is an intelligent, wild creature, and the process of making them subservient to humans for the purpose of being ridden is selfish, inhumane, and brutal.

My travels after leaving Jumpee empower and expand me in ways that are inexpressible. I know that I must return to Thailand prior to my flight back to Canada to thank her in person. It is a treat beyond words to stand before her, feeding her bunches of bananas. Her trunk sways and scoops up each bunch eagerly. I pat her rough skin, looking into her eye and talking to her without words. I do not ride her, but rather walk next to her on the way to the river. I watch with delight as she immerses herself several times in the water. It is a slow amble back down the pathway, and we pass other elephants on their way to the river.

I am now lagging behind since the *mahout* has her pick up the pace. She is now being taken to her bed for the night on a longer chain with lots of food next to her. Part of me is very sorrowful since this is goodbye. As I approach her, my heart sings as she now walks toward me of her own choice. I kiss her tenderly, whispering "I love you and shall see you again someday." She rumbles contentedly.

Carol Ann Joy Arnim is an adventuresome free spirit who follows the voice of her soul. She has trained five service dog puppies and traveled extensively. She is passionate about animals and volunteerism. Through her speaking and books, she inspires people to embrace their highest truth.

www.carolannjoyarnim.com

PATHWAY TO LASTING JOY

Nasrin Barbic

Your task is not to seek for love, but merely to seek and find all the barriers
within yourself that you have built against it.
RUMI

So often when we are in a search for happiness, we look outside of ourselves.
We search for the one who can make us happy, the perfect job, the perfect
friends, and so on. People often think their experiences are coming at them
from the outside in, but I've learned on my journey that our experiences
come through us from the inside out.

In May 2013, I woke up—in a seemingly perfect life—feeling unhappy
and confused. I had been married for ten years, had two wonderful boys, a
successful career of thirteen years as a software engineer, lived in a beautiful
house, and had no financial worries. And yet that morning I realized I was
living a lie. I felt disconnected from myself, my husband, and even my children.
I had done everything I was supposed to do. By all accounts I was successful,
but I still didn't know who I was or what I really wanted. All I knew at that
point was that I was not happy in my marriage or my job, and as much as I
adored my boys, I wasn't showing up for them either because often I was lost
in my thoughts. I felt as though I had been sleepwalking throughout my life.

Consequently, a year later I found myself in the middle of a divorce and
feeling miserable. I could not stop the chatter in my head, which told me my
husband and outside circumstances were to blame for the pain and sorrow I
was experiencing. Looking back, I realized I had felt unloved and heartbroken
before in my past relationships. The only difference this time was that I had
kids, and I couldn't easily walk away as I had done in the past.

I started seeing a pattern in my life, and I became determined to figure
out why I kept creating the same circumstances. My romantic relationships
always started with a love affair but ended with me feeling disconnected

and unloved. I decided to put my divorce on hold and focus on myself. My journey took me to yoga, meditation, life coaching, hypnotherapy, and energy healing, and what I learned in the process transformed my life.

Problem areas are a symptom of underlying hurts or limiting core beliefs; they are often unconscious but keep reasserting themselves in a variety of ways. Most of us carry emotional blockages. They can show up anywhere—in our relationships, at work, even in our body. These barriers can make us feel trapped in the same pattern over and over again, even when we're actively trying to change our lives. We often make choices and behave in ways that reinforce the very situations we don't want.

In my case, after going through hypnotherapy, I realized that because of my childhood circumstances and growing up among nine siblings, I felt invisible and unworthy of love. I had been totally unaware of this, but looking back, I realized how I had sabotaged my relationships because I felt I was not enough, not lovable, and not worthy of attention.

Until we honestly come to terms with our limiting core beliefs and why we make the choices we make, change cannot occur. We often use our energy to try to change the people or situations in our lives, but this action renders us feeling depleted, frustrated, and angry. Our focus is in the wrong place—change is an inside job!

I had to learn to love myself. Practicing yoga allowed me to manage my stress and anxiety. Through meditation, I was able to quiet the negative chatter and replace it with more empowering thoughts. With the help of my coach, I learned to recognize the limiting beliefs that were holding me back from living an empowered life. I connected with my inner child through hypnotherapy, and I guided my inner child through the healing process. I learned that unless we heal our inner child, our true self will not be able to fully emerge.

In 2015, after two years of separation, my husband and I decided to get back together. In the end, it looked as though nothing had changed. I still had the same job, lived in the same house, was married to the same man—and yet everything was different because I was not the same person. One day, as I was playing with my nine-year-old son, he looked deep into my eyes and said, "Mom, I love the way you are now; please don't go back to the way you used to be." I used to be stressed, lost in my thoughts, short-tempered, angry, and anxious. Now I was at peace, content, joyful, present, and in love with life and myself.

Through finding myself, I also discovered my purpose and passion in life. I became a certified life coach, hypnotherapist, and Reiki master. I quit my full-time job as a software engineer and I now dedicate myself to helping others:

1. Create a clear vision for what they want out of life so they know where they're going and why they're going there.
2. Remove the frustrating blocks and limiting beliefs that are holding them back and replace them with positivity and possibility.
3. Become empowered to step into the life they long to live and manage relationships, work, and life with joy and ease.

I believe we create our lives from the inside out—we create our reality based on what we believe about ourselves and the world around us, consciously or unconsciously. Your inner thoughts, beliefs, and feelings create everything you see and experience in your outer world. The more you focus on changing your inner reality, the faster you will see new and amazing results in your outer reality! *When you have nothing inside holding you back, there is nothing outside that can hold you back either.*

Nasrin Barbic is a certified life coach, hypnotherapist, Reiki master, and founder of Pathway to Lasting Joy. Nasrin blends traditional coaching methods, scientifically proven techniques, and deep healing through hypnotherapy and Reiki to help clients release mental, physical, and spiritual blocks to success in all areas of their life.

www.pathwaytolastingjoy.com

The Magic of a Bold Goal

Melanie Benson

What do you think you could achieve if you had the confidence to step into a more daring and bold version of yourself? An audacious goal? A bold vision? The ability to truly create a legacy and impact on this planet? The energy of a bold goal catapults you forward and ignites a more fulfilled and expansive you.

Maybe you have a mission that is so big you have no idea how to pull it off. A bold goal ignites your focus. Bold goals require you to become more resourceful, more confident, and more committed, ultimately challenging you to stretch beyond your comfort zone to become the person who can achieve any outcome.

If you have a bold goal in mind, you know what I mean. Your goal probably has been roaming around in your mind for some time now, evolving into something way bigger than you know how to pull off. It feels simultaneously inspiring and terrifying, but the thought of not pursuing the goal leaves you feeling unfulfilled. Yet you just can't get this idea into motion.

Maybe you can relate to one of these two scenarios:

1) You are determined to conquer your bold goal, so you commit and jump in. But you don't know what you're doing, so confusion kicks in. What steps should you take? You've never done this before, and you don't know anyone who has. Fears and doubts take over as you imagine all the ways this could become an epic fail. You could run out of money, perform miserably in front of your colleagues and friends, or ultimately lose everything you've worked so hard for. Now your previously inspired mind is in full-blown panic. Your logic mind chimes in, providing you with several rational and perfectly acceptable reasons that this idea is crazy. You decide to dump it and work on something more tangible and "safe."

2) You find yourself in a state of limbo. Your old goals no longer
   motivate you, and your thoughts are spinning as you try to find a
   new direction. You've pursued a few different paths, but nothing is
   lighting your fire. Bored, frustrated, and a bit disillusioned, you feel
   disenchanted with no clear vision of what's next. If you are a high
   achiever by nature, you're miserable because you pride yourself as
   someone who's always in motion. If you are more of a "slow and
   steady" person, this lull has pretty much taken you out of the game.
   Being caught in ambiguity has slowed you down to a full stop.

The second scenario was my story. I found myself a few years ago in
that state of limbo. Having accomplished great success, I had hit a wall
of uncertainty. Not feeling particularly inspired by any new direction, I
felt stuck. I knew I wasn't "done"—I just couldn't reignite my fire! Having
overcome so many limitations, this stage was frustrating and demoralizing.

But then I set a really bold goal. Instead of just trying to find the next step,
I went BIG. I set my sights on a level of success I had never achieved. Instead
of falling back on old patterns, I had to awaken a new level of leadership.
Connecting to a bold goal was my pivot point. I found opportunities rolling
in faster than I could keep up while revenues began to multiply again.

Let's look at how the power of a bold goal can help you pivot and ignite
new levels of success:

- A bold mindset dissolves fear and doubt that normally hold you back.
- The energy of a bold goal shakes away mental cobwebs for greater clarity.
- Confidence and courage soar through your body so you can take
  actions that you've been unwilling to take.
- Resources and million-dollar connections seem to magically appear.
- Influence, impact, and income expand exponentially with grace and ease.

Now, don't let one of the two biggest reasons smart, talented people fail
to achieve their goals derail you! Here's what they are:

1) "I Don't Have Time"—Time can be your greatest enemy; most
people fill their days with their current life priorities, ultimately
believing they never have enough time to pursue anything else. But
people who achieve their bold goals create time because their goal has
become their priority.

2) "I Don't Feel Capable"—When you want to do something you've never done before, doubts often cloud your thinking and you can start to believe that you aren't capable. Perhaps you don't know where the money will come from. The gap starts to widen, and the mental trash kicks into high gear.

In his book *The Magic of Thinking Big*, Dr. David Schwartz says, "Belief, strong belief, triggers the mind to figure out ways and means how to." When you believe fully in your bold goal, you activate the most resourceful part of you. Resources that seemed blocked before will become obvious. Obstacles will no longer stop you as you will be determined to find a way, no matter what. Belief is part of the Bold Goal Formula that shatters your limits and kicks your motivation into high gear.

Isn't it time to shatter your limits and really start making the impact you dream of? Whether you are an influential leader already or you have a compelling mission to make a greater impact, using the Bold Goal Formula will serve you for a lifetime. Decide you will go for your bold goal. Commit to becoming the person who can pull it off!

*Melanie Benson, host of Own Your Bold®
Challenge, is a Success Amplifier. She hosts
the* Amplify Your Success Podcast, *is author
of* Rewired for Wealth, *co-author of Entre-
preneur.com's* Start Up Guide to Starting an
Information Marketing Business, *and her
success tips are featured in* Bloomberg Business Week, Woman's Day, *and* Parenting
Magazine.

www.melaniebenson.com

Uniquely You

Ulrika Brattemark

At the tender age of twenty-four, I took a job at a software company in Gothenburg, Sweden. My plan was to work there for about a year while I figured out what I *really* wanted to do. I was young and ambitious, innately curious and eager to learn. Surely I would soon discover my path.

Fast-forward twenty-four years later: I found myself living on the other side of the world, with my own family, and having worked *half of my life* at the same company. Crazier still was that I had ended up in a career in tech! How did THAT happen?

At some point, however, about halfway into that career, I started to sense that something was missing. Although I was skilled at analyzing, organizing, and implementing systems and enjoyed many aspects of my work, at some deeper level I knew this was not THE career for me. I wanted to do work that mattered on a more personal level—to me as well as to others. I realized that a core part of me was being neglected.

Through a series of explorations, I began rediscovering these left-behind parts. At a workshop offered through my employer, I completed a values exercise. Not surprisingly, I identified my top value as "spending time with family and friends." The values that were tied for second place, however, provided my wake-up call. They were: "serving others" and "helping society." The facilitator of the workshop came over to look at my self-assessment. He leaned in, and uttered under his breath, as if afraid of being overheard: "I don't usually say this, but . . . um . . . you might want to look for a different career."

If I only knew what career that might be . . .

During the next several years, I continued to explore. I became really curious about what I was naturally good at, what I had a passion for, and what really made me come alive. At work, I volunteered for assignments that were outside of my actual job description but felt more aligned with my values. I took on an Employee Engagement Champion role, I co-organized a Leadership Forum, and I insisted I'd be part of a team that had formed to work in a new, dynamic, and collaborative way. I loved contributing in ways that helped my colleagues thrive.

Outside of work, I explored too. I read lots of books, attended multiple workshops, and even pursued a parallel career as a yoga teacher. Then one day, while browsing a catalog from my favorite retreat center, The Esalen Institute, I found a workshop on something called "coaching." Hmm . . . that sounded fascinating! I decided to check it out.

After the first two days in that coaching workshop, I was SOLD. Can you imagine? There is a *profession* that focuses on being in conversations about what deeply matters!

I finally had found my "sweet spot"—the intersection between my skills and my passions, with the potential of serving a need in the world.

Next, I embarked on a search of what specific need that might be. I discovered that nearly everyone I spoke with wanted help prioritizing the multitude of demands on their time. They no longer wanted to live life at such a frazzling pace. Some wanted to overcome procrastination. Practically everyone wanted to accomplish more of what was truly important. And I had the skills to help them!

After a few years of moonlighting as a coach, I took the leap and went out on my own. Finally, at the age of forty-eight, I had figured out what I really wanted to be "when I grow up."

As a time management coach, I am now able to leverage my organizational and analytical skills, as well as my innate curiosity about how we as humans work. I get to be in deep conversation with others, helping them discover and implement ways to spend their time on what most matters to them.

Now, over to you: *What's YOUR sweet spot?*

- **What are you really good at?** Take inventory of your skills, experiences, and knowledge. It's easy to take for granted that which comes easily to us, so make sure you ask your friends, family, and colleagues for input. Then OWN that expertise.
- **What makes you come alive?** What brings you deep joy and fulfillment? For what topic do you have an infinite appetite? What activities give you more energy? Start doing more of what makes you come ALIVE.

- **Show up as fully as you can.** Explore ways to more fully leverage your skills. Choose activities and assignments that better align with your values and your passion. Stay curious about which need in the world you are meant to meet. The world needs you to be *UNIQUELY YOU.*

It may not take decades to discover, but even if it does, those explorations are all part of your life's journey. Make sure you stay in discovery mode, and your self-awareness will increase. Let that self-awareness inform your daily decisions, in alignment with your values and dreams. On a daily basis, allow more time for that which fills your soul. What small action, that lights you up, can you take today? Many tiny little steps add up and make a difference.

Whether you change careers or not, find a new hobby or revive an old one, my wish for you is that you honor your natural strengths, your core values, and your deepest desires. I believe that every person that claims their uniqueness and shares their brilliance in this world helps create a better world for all. Supporting others in doing just that is my contribution, and it makes ME come alive!

The way you live your DAYS is the way you end up living your LIFE. Choose carefully!

Ulrika Brattemark is a Corporate Swede on a Soulful Mission. As a time management coach, speaker, and workshop leader, she supports busy professionals in living sane, joyful, and fulfilling lives. She encourages her clients to incorporate their dreams into their daily lives, ultimately actualizing a life that is truly theirs.

www.coachulrika.com

The Strength in Adversity

Vanessa Caraveo

"Success is not measured by what you accomplish but by the opposition you have encountered, and the courage with which you have maintained the struggle against overwhelming odds."
Orison Swett Marden

We can't deny that there is a strength built in those who overcome adversity. Hardship often prepares ordinary people for an extraordinary destiny. It tests us to become stronger and to face things head on—to not live on the surface and to dig that much deeper. Nothing worth having comes easy, and nothing worth reaching for comes without setbacks. But it is the inner strength we discover in ourselves through persevering against the adversity we face that helps us discover and live up to our fullest potential.

My journey began when, at birth, my mother received a dire prognosis for me from her doctor. I was diagnosed with a medical condition, and the doctor said there was a high probability I wouldn't be able to walk, might not make it past my adolescent years, and if I did, would have profound learning disabilities. A lifelong road of challenges ahead awaited me that would definitely put into play, not only my own personal discipline and determination, but also my family's unconditional love and faith.

Growing up, I realized that by not placing limits on myself and focusing on what I could do, I would be able to move forward with fortitude and accomplish anything I set my mind to. With hard work, determination, and perseverance, I was able overcome the many challenges life presented me, never allowing any adversity to limit me in reaching my goals and turning my dreams into reality. Despite the not-very-high expectations others placed on me, my mother's faith in me remained strong, and she was able to have me walking at ten months of age. I was able to survive my adolescent years, truly blessed to have graduated high school early at sixteen years old. Education has always been a significant part of my life, and it has been an important stepping-stone for achieving many extraordinary things. This served as motivation to stay on top of my academics, and I graduated college with honors and went on to become one of only two nationally board-certified professionals for my field in South Texas, allowing me to make a difference in many lives.

I knew in my heart that I wanted to use my experiences to help others facing similar challenges in their journey. Throughout the years, I have had the great privilege of being a member, volunteer, and sponsor for various disability organizations and nonprofit groups, and I also was designated as an official disability ambassador for my state of Texas, where I am passionate and dedicated to raising disability awareness and promoting inclusion for all individuals. In today's society, we continue to recognize that considerable change is still needed when it comes to inclusion and acceptance—not only for those with disabilities, but also for individuals of different nationalities. We need to come to the realization that only when we truly accept others for who they are can we grow as a society and also equally benefit from one another as a whole. Empathy and a greater understanding for others of all walks of life should be emphasized, and we can learn a great deal from one another when we do not close ourselves off from those who are different than us. Instead we must realize that we are all human and are all God's children designed uniquely to share with one another and help each other in our own special way on this journey called life.

I discovered my love for writing in elementary school, when I realized it was a great outlet to express myself. Throughout the years I entered writing and poetry contests and did very well. We all have dreams in life, and since childhood, mine was to someday become an award-winning author. With much hard work and patience, I was able to turn this dream into a reality, and I have published various books and poems with a focus on making a positive difference in others' lives.

The future lies with our youth, and I firmly believe that children need positive role models and good examples to learn from and be inspired by; these are more effective than just words. I enjoy sharing my award-winning book with youth about embracing their differences and letting their inner light always shine bright, sharing the message that they can accomplish anything they set their mind to. I also take time out to promote literacy for youth at schools, libraries, and community events, and I am a member of many organizations that promote both reading and writing.

I also was inspired by my personal experience to write an inspirational novel which raises disability awareness as well as the importance inclusion plays in today's society with the hope that this story would inspire others to never stop believing in themselves and the power we all possess within us to turn our dreams into reality and defy any adversity in life. As an inspirational speaker for schools, church and faith groups, and various other organizations, I enjoy sharing my personal story and message with others of how my unrelenting faith and determination helped me to be where I am today.

When we share our personal light with others, we have the power to make a positive difference in this world and in the lives of others. I know the adversity I have faced helped to make me the person I am today, for which I am thankful. By believing in ourselves, we can rise above any challenge and scale any hurdle in our way. Our spontaneous reactions to any challenge will go a long way in defining how resounding our success eventually turns out. If we persevere, bide our time, and buckle down to do what is necessary, we will succeed in living up to our fullest potential.

Vanessa Caraveo is an award-winning author, published poet, and inspirational speaker who has a passion for promoting inclusion for all and helping others discover the power within them to overcome adversity. She was awarded the Inspirational Woman of the Year Award and aspires to continue making a positive difference in many lives.

My Life, My Terms

Natasha Clawson

My corporate job came to an abrupt, screaming halt in January 2019.

I'd been with this particular company for roughly four years, during which I'd rapidly climbed the ladder from executive admin all the way to a director-level position.

As the company grew and changed, I found that although I was in alignment with their purpose-driven mission, other values that mattered deeply to me had become incongruent. Try as I might, I no longer fit within the organization.

However, I couldn't seem to move forward. Should I go back into business for myself (I had been a freelance designer), or should I find another corporate position? In my heart, I knew I wanted to pursue entrepreneurship . . . but I was afraid. When I had worked for myself previously, I had hustled so hard that I eventually burned myself out. I had experienced massive anxiety resulting from improper boundaries and a lack of experience and resources.

At this point, I felt recharged and equipped to leave, but that self-doubt lingered. I continued to waffle on the decision, all the while becoming more and more miserable at work. Eventually I had a very open conversation with leadership about the lack of alignment I felt, and what had led up to this divide. This resulted in my abrupt termination.

Years ago, this conversation would have been devastating, earth-shattering, and insurmountable. In fact, it never would have happened. I was raised to *never* give any indication of being unhappy at a job. If you were leaving, you didn't tell them until you had another job and your two-weeks' notice in hand.

But in the four years that I had been with this company, I had learned a lot about honest conversations, and I'm not someone who holds back—even at the cost of a job. I also learned that turnover doesn't have to be a bad thing. I had seen countless people leave a position they didn't love and go on to do wonderful things somewhere else!

So many people (myself included) get overly attached to a job. It is easy to become so invested in the identity you build there, or the dependence on a paycheck—or even your family or spouse's expectations of who and what you should be—that you lose sight of what's *right* for you.

I know I delayed leaving because I was worried about the expectations of my friends and family, especially the opinion of my fiancé. Our financial obligations didn't make this any easier. We had just bought our first house (in California, no less!) and were still in full-throttle saving mode for our fast-approaching wedding.

Despite my concerns, my family and fiancé were more supportive than I could have envisioned. The timing was perfect, and leaving my corporate job opened up doors for me that had been inaccessible before. My creativity blossomed, and I felt the weight of exhaustion that I had been carrying around lift. When I felt that lightness, I knew I was back on my path. I could be nothing but thankful for the circumstances that had led me to this point.

I still wish I had had the courage and trust in myself to leave my corporate job when I realized there was no future there. It would have saved me months of pain.

Maybe if we weren't so afraid of the stigma of leaving a job or being let go, we'd have more honest conversations sooner and help people who aren't in the right place get to the *right* destination faster, instead of spending months or years *trapped* in a job they dislike.

A Gallup poll reported that 70 percent of people in the United States aren't engaged in their jobs.[1] That's insane! Especially since these people are waking up every day and *choosing* to go to this job. We're not indentured servants—but sometimes we act like it.

If you're where I was, I've got news for you: you don't have to wait! You're in control of your life and your choices.

No matter what other people think, this is *your* life. And if you aren't happy somewhere, then it's time to evaluate what's going on and fix it or make a change. Only *you* have that power in your life. **No one else is going to do it for you.**

Let's quit being so damn afraid. Let's be open to changing as many times and as often as we need to. The path of life is not linear—it's a journey of constant growth, enlightenment, and discovery.

And just so we're clear, I'm not saying that everyone should be an entrepreneur. Sometimes I wonder if it's right for me!

And that's OK. You should constantly be evaluating, changing, and evolving. What was right yesterday may not be right today. If you stop holding on to what you think you must be, and instead be willing to flow with what is true for yourself, you will experience a higher level of fulfillment.

This approach to life is starting a new wave in business. Together, we're creating the modern workplace where work and life are no longer separate, but integral.

We are building a supportive and encouraging workplace and world where *every single one of us beautiful, magical human beings* can feel loved and accepted. We all have a perfect fit and we need to help each other discover it.

Whether it's telling yourself to move on, or helping someone else along their path, let this story serve as your inspiration. Wherever you are, be there intentionally. Don't get stuck somewhere because of your expectations of how things "should" be.

You only have this one life, so *live* it on your terms.

1. https://news.gallup.com/opinion/chairman/212045/world-broken-workplace.aspx?g_source=position1&g_medium=related&g_campaign=tiles.

Natasha Clawson is a graphic designer and brand enthusiast. She helps businesses create visual brand identities with a sense of clarity and composure that positions them for growth. She's a proud millennial and tireless champion of healthy workplace culture and mental health.

www.aspireenco.com

Core Purpose: The Tiniest Matryoshka Doll

Deb Coman

To see her today, you would be hard-pressed to envision the carefree, lighthearted, chatty person she always was. Unless, of course, you could see beyond the physical challenges the years saved up and bombarded her with all at once. If you (as my sisters and dad and I) had connected with the essence of her before now, you'd close your eyes and bring back her vibrant personality to this silent body in a nursing home. It's what we do. It's the only thing we can do.

What is it that makes us who we are even when our bodies betray us? What is our essence underneath the surface? How do we get there and preserve it?

Beyond her body, even beyond her quiet eyes, she is still there. She is still Mom. The essence of her is in there, somewhere. And for now, it has to be enough. Our souls know each other, even without conversation. We all remain connected.

But what is this essence that makes her "her"? Clearly not the body that doesn't work the way it did all the years before. And not the voice, now unheard most days. Her heart remains strong in spite of its partner parts and systems no longer doing their jobs. Her spirit remains. The connection to that is strong. Her inner strength and will are palpable, even on the darkest of days.

Our essence is more than how our bodies show up. It is more than our voice; it's more than how we engage in the world. It often lives beyond the grasp of our language. Though we feel it in our hearts and minds, we fumble to describe it in words. When we name it, our reward is the connection that it brings . . . the connection beyond our physical presence.

Stripping away the layers to reveal our own core doesn't come naturally.

There's a tug of war between wanting to know what's in there and not wanting everyone else to see. It takes time and help to entice it into the light. We must feel safe and still be brave.

The words we'll eventually choose to talk about our essence do matter. The nuances of their meaning are important. In my strategy work with business owners to hone their messaging and content, defining their core message and values is step one. Uncovering the core is slippery and elusive at first. It requires excavation and a willingness to go deep.

Why we do what we do and who we really are—our core purpose—is central to everything that follows. It's impossible and unwise to build a house on a flimsy foundation. As business owners, speakers, authors . . . as people . . . all our language comes from this. When we define ourselves and our work through a website, an email, an article, or a talk, it comes from our core message.

If you haven't identified this core in language that captures it clearly, your foundation is not solid. Alignment in your message is critical to establish trust. It's essential for consistent connection with the people you intend to reach. It's the thread that ties all of what you do and who you are together. It's a language that speaks beyond the body.

Exploring core messaging for business owners is an honor that fills my soul with joy and my eyes with tears at times. Using a process that fosters safety, connection, and ease, I'm in awe of what's uncovered each time I do this. Helping someone to see her or his own essence, often in a new light and with new language, is truly a privilege.

Uncovering core messaging involves repeatedly asking why as we go deeper into the layers and label what emerges. The process is similar to a matryoshka—a Russian nesting, or babushka, doll where each wooden doll has another smaller one within it. As we shed the outer layers, we eventually arrive at a small, yet mighty core . . . the tiniest matryoshka doll. She defines our core essence.

In my own un-nesting of the dolls, I began with the largest matryoshka: I helped business owners write and edit their messaging. Why? Because clear messaging is critical to effective communication. But there was a smaller matryoshka within: to create messages that attract and compel the right people to buy. Why? Because clear messaging has intention. And then, a smaller matryoshka still: strategy in messaging to share and repurpose it. Why? Because intention needs a specific action plan. And still then, the tiniest matryoshka: to create meaningful connection between you and your customers. Again, why? Because people buy from people, and *you* are the essence of your business. It is only through communicating your true, real core that you can stand out in a sea of online noise.

Your why is my why. I desperately want your message to reach the people you're meant to serve. I want your business and your life to thrive. When you do, I do too. And my teeny, tiniest matryoshka is to live the life that fills my heart with joy and inspires me, one that gives me time, prosperity, and meaningful experiences with my family.

The tiniest matryoshka that lives inside my mom still shows. I witness her strength. She has endured physical discomfort and body function betrayal more painful and long-lasting than many of us ever will. In spite of it all, her will to live, her spirit, and her inspiration is stronger than all her challenges combined. I see you, tiniest matryoshka. I see you.

May you have a person and a process to excavate your core essence and communicate it with the world. It will strengthen you in your purpose and become a beacon that attracts the right people you're meant to serve. Without one, you are untethered. Once revealed, your tiniest matryoshka will bring you clarity, connection, and all the success you can imagine. It would be my honor to share your journey.

Deb Coman is a content conversion strategist, copywriter, and speaker. Her copy is behind some of the big-name Facebook™ ads you see, and her strategies power many blogs, social media sites, and email campaigns. By aligning with core values, Deb supports business owners to attract and convert through connection.

www.debcoman.com

CELEBRATING TEN YEARS OF BEING CANCER-FREE

Tracey Ehman

As we rang in 2020 and entered the roaring 20s, I took time to reflect on the past decade. It brought with it so many unexpected experiences.

In 2010 I was healthy and had no idea what the world had in store for me. Then, one day in April, I felt a lump. It's a crazy feeling when you know you know. And my journey with breast cancer began.

Throughout the next year, I experienced a number of emotions, went through surgery, healing, chemo, hair loss, radiation, and learning to embrace this new version of myself. At times it was hard for sure, but I truly tried not to concentrate on the sickness or the side effects from treatment. Instead I focused on making memories and keeping life as normal as possible. I didn't miss a single event during my chemo. I made it to my annual Christmas party, celebrated Christmas, and even rang in 2011 with friends at a New Year's party two days after my last chemo session.

Looking back, it was definitely a hard time and yet, while cancer doesn't define me, it has brought about new experiences that I would have never imagined in my wildest dreams. I was able to triple my business while going through chemo, and I still have 90 percent of those clients with me today. I have now become an international bestselling author, sharing my story "You Have the Power to Rise Above" in *Voices of the 21st Century: Women Who Influence, Inspire, and Make a Difference* and "How Your Story Can Turn into a Movement" in *Voices of the 21st Century: Bold, Brave, and Brilliant Women Who Make a Difference*—as well as my own book *The Silver Lining of Cancer* featuring twelve other women who share their story of how cancer impacted their life.

In *The Silver Lining of Cancer*, I wanted to help people concentrate on all the good, even if it is just a sliver of hope. Bringing these stories together brought healing to those wonderful women who shared their stories, and many said it was a cathartic experience. I also experienced this when I first shared my story in the first *Voices of the 21st Century*. There is so much power in being able to embrace, share, and learn from your story, and it's amazing the impact your story can have on other people's lives as well.

These stories touch on self-healing; letting go of negativity; embracing memories; advocating for screening and genetics; unexpected lessons learned; making memories; welcoming the memories made; and the power of community and paying it forward with hope.

Below is an excerpt from my original chapter in *Voices of the 21st Century: Women Who Influence, Inspire, and Make a Difference.*

For me, looking for the positive and not concentrating on the negative was key to my healing. Being an entrepreneur, I wasn't sent home from a corporate job, put on sick leave, and left to dwell on what the Universe was doing to me. Instead I was concentrating on helping clients, achieving great things, and spending time with my family.

During this time of treatment, I was thrilled to be involved in a project that is near and dear to my heart: Women Speakers Association. The opportunity to develop and build the first version of WSA's website kept me centered. It gave me an opportunity to keep my mind fresh and be inspired by women who wanted to make a difference for other women globally. Through this process and support, many of these women have become the closest of friends, mentors, and people I just couldn't do without in my life.

I chose to rise above and embrace the "glass is half full" scenario, rather than dwell on the "what ifs." We all have to deal with roadblocks along the way—some small, some larger than life—but by focusing on what you do want versus what you don't, you can positively impact your outcome in life, business, and success.

My journey through diagnosis, healing, and embracing my life fully in the past decade has allowed me to make a difference is so many people's lives, and for that I am grateful. Here is one of the reviews I received after *The Silver Lining of Cancer* was published:

This is one of the most moving books I have ever read in my life. I have seen a side of cancer that I wouldn't wish on anyone. One where there was no coming back because within a month of diagnosis my mother was gone in a blink of an eye. She fought the fight like these women did, but she lost. Reading these women's stories revealed a whole different side of cancer where there is beautiful hope, strength, and courage. These women fought the biggest fight of their life, and they won. They are fierce and amazing and so inspiring. I honestly think this is the best the book I have read in a long time. There is nothing more beautiful than a strong and fierce woman!

The resounding success of *The Silver Lining of Cancer* and the impact it has already had makes me feel empowered to help more people to share their stories, their messages of hope. I am pleased to be introducing a new podcast series later this year called *Silver Lining Conversations*. This podcast, like my book, will concentrate on helping people to share their silver lining of cancer. I envision that this will be a place where people can share their stories of hope, inspiration, joy, gratitude, and love.

If you would like to apply to be a guest on my podcast, or get a copy of my book, please visit TheSilverLiningofCancer.com. If you are reading this and are interested in being a sponsor, you can contact me through the website as well.

Wishing you health, happiness, and abundance in 2020 and beyond!

Tracey Ehman is a bestselling author of The Silver Lining of Cancer *and a social media strategist who tripled her business while battling cancer. Her ability to concentrate on the positive, even in adversity, compelled her to bring together others to share their stories and inspire people to look for the silver lining.*

www.thesilverliningofcancer.com

THE JOY WITHIN

Grace Gapuz

Are you interested in finding more profound joy in life? I'm assuming you are; otherwise you would have skipped this chapter. I have learned that joy is an inside job. It is the desire of every human being. It is a positive emotion that stems from a conscious possession of a good or the fulfillment of a desire.

Finding joy comes when we make peace with who we are, why we are, and how we are. Such joy boosts our energy in a way that makes us feel good about what we're doing, the challenges ahead of us, and how we look at ourselves.

The ongoing search for joy is a journey leading to a true model of life, of hope, and of faith. Nobody wishes to be stressed, confused, stuck, or lost. If you are experiencing moments of anxiety, loneliness, failure, disappointment, or rejection, I'm here to tell you there is hope in this world.

In this chapter I will share pointers I have used myself that you can apply to lead you in finding continued joy and to successfully relish the wonderful gift of life you have been given.

Joy is one of the greatest gifts I have had in life since childhood. My heart overflows with gratitude for parents who raised me with unconditional love. They taught me values through their good examples. They kept me grounded. I was also surrounded by other people who loved and cared for me. All of these provided the stamina for me to move forward in my life and keep dreaming of new adventures and climbing new mountains.

My life has been an ongoing journey of changes and choices. It was not all smooth and light over the years. I've faced challenges about my priorities, career, and yes, letting go of my children to college and beyond. I doubted my future and feared I might face failure, hardship, emptiness, and pain along the way. But with these challenges, I began to find that hope was becoming more real. My faith in God grew stronger, and it served as my primary inspiration. His blessed presence in my life consoled me and granted me the courage to persevere.

Below are the top keys I've learned about finding the joy within. I hope they will inspire you to live your joy too!

Be grateful for big and small blessings. Gratitude is a choice. I have learned to practice writing a list of things that happened for which I am grateful each day. It boosts my energy and my ability to feel more positive, confident, and open to other people. It can be as simple as saying aloud "I enjoyed my walk today." In our thankfulness, true earthly joy resides.

Cultivate humility and embrace it. This is the foundation for a life of happiness and joy. How can it be obtained? It is not an easy task, but the rewards are amazing! It is a process requiring surrender and detachment by allowing your desires and fears to become transformed by God. When you allow this, you will begin to discover freedom from tendencies of selfishness and gaining the esteem of others. You will find your worth in God and how He sees you. Rick Warren said, "Humility is not thinking less of yourself; it's thinking of yourself less."

Seek healing. We all need to feel safe and secure. Let go of the past events in your life. We all have wounds, and we all need help in healing our broken sense of self. Get rid of your feelings of low self-esteem that cause you to judge yourself and others. Your future starts today. Remember that you can begin again with God's help.

Pray. Find materials that speak of peace, hope, and truth. Meditate on them. Contemplate on the words of hope from Christ Himself in the Sacred Scriptures and allow them to come alive. What are those words telling you? Do they reinforce your confidence and calm you down? Praying helps create a frame of mind that will allow you to move forward to the next step. Be trusting, confident, persistent, and unafraid in prayer.

Share your joy. "God loves a cheerful giver. Bring that love and joy into the world of today . . . Joy, to be fruitful, has to be shared." (Mother Teresa of Calcutta)

Stay connected with supportive people and seek out a trusted network or group. Do not isolate yourself. Others need you, and you need them, too, but choose to stay with those who accept you unconditionally. Detach when loyalty is inappropriate. Healthy connections bring joy and give you a genuine sense of belongingness.

Structure your time and goals; pursue what you have intended. Have a commitment to your intentions. Take some time to think and prioritize to know where you are and where you would like to go. Make a to-do list with your priorities at the top. Keep your eyes open to new opportunities. Be focused, persistent, and turn off distractions. Doing whatever it takes to reach your goal leads to joy.

Take charge of your well-being. Remain open to and aware of what's happening in you and around you. Look for practical ideas that help you feel better and start building a joyful life. Sit back, take a deep breath, and appreciate the things that are going well in your life. And don't forget to find the sources of joy. These can be felt, seen, lived, and shared with others.

Serenity Prayer

God grant me the serenity to accept the things I cannot change;
The courage to change the things I can
And the wisdom to know the difference.
Living one day at a time;
enjoying one moment at a time;
accepting hardship as a pathway to peace;
Taking, as Jesus did, this sinful world as it is,
not as I would have it;
Trusting that You will make things
right if I surrender to Your will
That I may be reasonably happy in this life
and supremely happy with You forever in the next. Amen.

Grace Gapuz, RN, CLNC, works as a certified legal nurse consultant and director of a dental practice. Grace holds a BS in Nursing and an MA in Organizational Management. She has authored a book, Medical Records Made Easy for Attorneys. *Grace volunteers with her church's spiritual ministries.*

www.gracegapuzlnc.com

WORKING TO END RACIAL INEQUALITY

Verenice Gutierrez, PhD

My world came to a screeching halt in the early afternoon of Saturday, August 3rd, 2019. My twenty-seven-year-old, six months-pregnant baby sister was on lockdown inside the Sam's Club in East El Paso with her baby boy and her partner. They were there to buy ice cream for my nephew's first birthday party when the massacre began at the Walmart next door. Several people had rushed into the Sam's Club when the shots started, and my sister did not know if the shooter was in the Sam's Club with them. Less than twenty-four hours before his first birthday, my baby nephew was experiencing his first lockdown.

The next several hours were tense. I obsessed over Twitter, the national news, and our family chat. I learned that the city I love was in deep mourning due to a calculated massacre fueled by hate for the people I love, that look like me, that are me. Until we learned that the shooter had surrendered, I worried that he, too, had rushed into Sam's during the chaos and would start shooting people in there as well. I was upset that my little sister had to evacuate holding her hands in the air to prove she was harmless while a police officer held her baby. I sobbed the day the list of victims was published. I felt guilty that I was happy the list did not include the names Anna B. Gutierrez, Kaleb V. Reyes, and baby boy Reyes. However, each of the twenty two victims' names represents multiple lives changed forever by a national climate that supports hate towards specific groups of people of color.

Addressing equity and access is what I do. It is in my title: Director of Educational Equity and Access. I advocate for historically marginalized groups. I train others to build their capacity to create inclusive spaces where all children can learn and thrive. I talk about critical race theory, micro-aggressions, and stereotype threat in predominantly white spaces with a hypervigilance of the potential impact of my words on their fragile psyches. Above all, in doing this work, I feel equity fatigue. The El Paso massacre was too personal. It was too close to home. It was the proverbial slap to my face, and I was ready to quit. However, I am not a quitter. There have been other times I could have broken down, but I did not. I have not. And I will not.

I was introduced to the field of racial equity in 2007 through a training for school administrators in the Portland Public School District. What I learned that day explained so many of my experiences that I was instantly hooked. I learned as much as I could and quickly became a "racial equity warrior." I will admit that in my initial zeal, I was very much a bull in a china shop. I unnerved many people with my passion to begin interrupting systemic racism and systems of oppression. I was dubbed an "aggressive" Latina. I also became a "reverse" racist who hated all white people. When the students in the Latino club I had started at my middle school outperformed the white students on all academic measures, the white PTA board demanded to know how much school money had been spent on the club. I took great pleasure in informing them that I had spent zero school funds but hundreds of my own. If they wanted to reimburse me, I had receipts. The stupefied look on their faces gave me great pleasure.

In 2010, I was selected for my first principalship. Having learned from my initial missteps, I was more strategic about my implementation of racial equity work but no less relentless. On my first day as a principal, one of my middle-aged, white female teachers barged into my office, wagging her finger in my face as she proclaimed that I was "shitting on the Mexicans." I was confounded as I looked at my caramel-colored skin, my office décor, and pictures of my family confirming that I was still of Mexican descent and had not somehow "shit" on my own people. I asked that teacher to meet with me, advising her she would want to bring her union rep.

By 2012, my little school was morphing into the equitable space I had dreamed of creating. That year we created a drumming core for our most at-risk black and brown boys. A core group of white teachers were not happy with the focus on our marginalized communities. They called the media, who ran a story on our equity work. When the reporter called to follow up on our work, I immediately activated her white fragility, and it had disastrous ramifications. The far, far-right media ran with the distorted story. Bill O'Reilly featured me on his "Patriots or Pinheads" segment. He and Greg Gutfeld decided I was a communist pinhead who hates peanut butter. The irony is that I really do dislike peanut butter, but not for the reasons they claimed. I received death threats via both email and snail mail. Our phone system crashed because of the volume of phone calls.

I have found myself struggling to engage in racial equity work because of the reminders of how close racial hate came to changing my life forever. I feel exhaustion, frustration, and occasional hopelessness in the work I do. Then I do some self-care and get over it. I know that my life's purpose is to continue to dismantle systemically oppressive educational systems. Reminders of my why come often through Facebook messenger in the form of pictures and videos of the beautiful next generation of my family. The historically marginalized students that are served within my current district are someone's why, and they deserve to attend schools where they are valued, encouraged, and empowered—and where conditions have been created for them to thrive. Given the amount of work to be done, it's time to get to work.

Verenice Gutierrez, PhD, has engaged school districts nationally in creating systems that focus on educational equity. Her focus is on changing systems that disadvantage historically marginalized groups. She currently serves as the director of Educational Equity for the Salt Lake City School District and consults with various school districts across the country.

www.drverenicegutierrez.com

STEP OUT, STEP IN, STEP UP

Charmaine Hammond

Life is full of moments: moments that define you. Moments that shape you. Moments that challenge you. And moments that help you grow.

Do you recall as a child what you wanted to be when you grew up?

Did you have a big dream that lit you up?

Some of you may have been like me, changing your grown-up plans and dreams, and some of you may have become exactly what you decided when you were young. Both are perfect outcomes.

As a painfully shy child, I wonder now if my parents ever imagined I would become a professional speaker and entrepreneur. They may have suspected I would become an author because I loved books, being read to, and writing. Maybe they did believe I would become a speaker. After all, I spent hours playing school after being at school.

I grew up in an entrepreneurial family with loving parents, great storytellers, two incredible sisters, strong family connections, and the encouragement to pursue my own path.

That path led me to become a correctional officer. Yup! I worked in jails. At four foot eleven and three-quarter inches, I didn't look like the "typical" jail guard. I had short, spiky blonde hair, a big heart, and a desire to make a difference. This ten-year career working with some of the most challenging adult and youth offenders taught me so much, including the ability to ask for help, be humble, recognize that everyone has a story, and realize that who they are in a particular moment may not be who that person actually is. This career taught me perseverance, the power of kindness, and how to cope with failure and painful learning experiences (there were many).

Ten years after I left the correctional system, I returned to school to earn a BA and then a master's degree in Conflict Analysis and Management.

I had worked as a counselor, the leader of a youth/teen drop-in center, the executive director of a women's crisis shelter, a program director of a psychiatry unit, a contract negotiation specialist for government—and then I was called . . . to step out.

I stepped out of a career I enjoyed that paid well, offered security, and provided me with ongoing learning. But it did not give me a sense of purpose.

Have you ever felt like something was missing? A sense that there was a bigger purpose for you, even if you didn't know what that was?

Purpose was the one piece missing in my puzzle of life. The rest of (or at least most of) the puzzle pieces were there. I had a loving family and husband, incredible friends, a social life, hobbies that gave me joy, and the list goes on. The missing piece was purpose.

Leaving my stable career and venturing into the instability of the entrepreneur world resulted in more roadblocks than I ever expected. However, even in the most challenging moments I never once thought about stepping back. I had stepped in—stepped into my purpose. I opened my first business, a dispute resolution company as I had become a chartered mediator. It grew to a team of five in less than two years, and then I opened my second business, an employment services company that employed five staff members. Now, I might be biased here, but I had the best teams a leader could want.

I clearly remember the day I was called to step in again. A corporate client had asked me to provide their team with some dispute resolution training and help their human resources department set up their internal policies and conflict resolution programs. For the first time in a long time, I was nervous. I didn't trust that I could deliver what I agreed to deliver.

But the moment I stood in front of those twenty team members, all eyes on me, I felt at home. I remember thinking, "*This* is what being on purpose is."

I stepped in. Speaking became my new joy—my new purpose.

Very quickly the speaking side of my business grew, and I mediated less and less; I had a highly capable and committed team to provide that service. I eventually changed my business model to focus purely on speaking, which I now have been doing for many years. My husband and I decided to move out of the community we were living in, resulting in more key decisions.

Moving from having two incredible teams, two offices, and two businesses to becoming a solopreneur was a big change. I found myself seeking opportunities to partner with other businesses or organizations, to collaborate with them on projects, products, or programs.

Collaboration lights me up.

In the process of stepping into these big life and business changes, I found myself quickly being invited to step up—to step up and support projects that matter, be a part of movements that make a difference, and utilize collaboration to create bigger impacts . . . which is the mission of Raise a Dream, a business I co-founded with my business partner Rebecca Kirstein.

As I reflect on the past thirty-plus years of stepping out, stepping in, and stepping up, there are three threads woven throughout, almost as if stitched together to support my purpose: kindness, collaboration, and courage.

Kindness is not just about how you show up and treat others. Kindness means giving, including giving kindness to ourselves. Kindness has the ability to transform relationships and lives, and it creates a ripple effect of more kindness.

Collaboration can inspire creativity, make the load lighter to carry, and create results not possible on your own. We always say, "It takes a team to raise your dream."

Courage is necessary for growth, change, stepping out, stepping in, and stepping up.

Life is full of moments: moments that define you. Moments that shape you. Moments that challenge you. And moments that help you grow.

The question is: How will you spend your moments?

Charmaine Hammond is a highly sought-after business keynote and workshop speaker. She is a business owner who teaches the importance of developing trust, healthy relationships, and collaboration in the workplace. Charmaine has helped corporate clients build resilient, engaged teams, develop high trust/accountability relationships, and solve the tough people issues that impact success.

www.charmainehammond.com

THE GREATEST GIFT

Lucky Lauridsen, RN

I could never have predicted that a quick stop at Walmart would break my heart.

It happened on a day when I was short on time. I whipped through the aisles, gathered my items, and stood in the checkout line.

The minutes were flying by, but the line was standing still. I started to feel frustrated. Why wasn't this line moving? I leaned over and looked to the front to see what was causing the delay.

That's when I saw an elderly lady at the till. I could tell she was struggling to hear the young cashier, because she was leaning in close to try and understand her. The cashier was evidently becoming annoyed. She rudely shrugged her shoulders and rolled her eyes in response to her customer's requests to repeat her words.

Then I noticed the customer was having difficulty getting money out of her wallet. It was obvious she was getting anxious and embarrassed with all eyes in the line upon her.

The other customers were restless and impatient and started grumbling. I heard one say to another, "Why don't old people shop when we're at work? They have all day!"

Then the disoriented cashier, not knowing what to do, quickly turned to the customers and apologized. She said nothing to the older lady.

Finally, the purchase was complete. The groceries were bagged, the change was given. The elderly lady gripped her walker. As she stepped away, she apologized to the clerk for being a big nuisance and wasting everyone's time. Then she shuffled away, looking sad and dejected.

That's when my heart broke. I felt so upset by how this woman had been treated.

As an observer of the interaction, it was obvious to me that the older woman was having hearing difficulties, and the reason she had struggled getting money out of her purse was likely because she had dexterity issues, as do many older adults. I had noticed that the lady had abnormally enlarged knuckles on both hands (most likely arthritis). If I had been able to see this from the back of the line, why hadn't the clerk noticed?

Walking out of the store, I started thinking about all the other times I had witnessed difficult or embarrassing situations between frontline staff and aging customers in a variety of settings such as banks, restaurants, and offices. My mind continued spinning as I drove home, going over a multitude of stories I had heard from friends and family.

The one that really stood out was a story from my friend Jan about her eighty-year-old mother. This lady is a social butterfly and very independent, although she walks with a cane. She went to meet friends at a popular restaurant for a birthday celebration. She was the first to arrive. The young hostess directed her to a high bar stool to sit while she waited for her friends. She cheerfully complied and precariously got herself seated on the stool, only minutes later falling off and breaking her hip. Ironically, the ambulance arrived at the same time as her friends.

Yet again there was an obvious clue—if an older person is walking with a cane, they have a mobility issue. Directing them to sit at a high bar stool is not a safe or reasonable option. How could the hostess not know this?

That's when I had my *aha!* moment.

In an instant it became clear to me that the needs and challenges of older seniors are often invisible to those with an untrained eye. There is a broad problem across many organizations of disconnection between frontline employees and older customers, which leaves them feeling undervalued and underserved. Often employees seem to be unaware of obvious struggles many older seniors experience on a daily basis, giving the impression of a lack of caring, empathy, or respect.

As a professional with decades of firsthand experience working with seniors, what I came to realize was that many people outside of the healthcare profession do not have the right knowledge or training around aging. They don't always recognize the emotional or physical problems many seniors experience or understand that they age differently.

I knew in that moment that if we provided the right training, employees would start to see things through a different lens, and it would transform the way they approach everyday interactions with older customers. The result would be more positive outcomes for both seniors and employees.

That incident in Walmart inspired me to create a solution that would support both seniors and employees. I felt a responsibility to help make a difference by sharing my knowledge and raise awareness about the challenges many seniors experience, so I created the Senior Awareness and Sensitivity Skills Training Certificate program, in an effort to assist staff and seniors.

Why is it so vital to do this now?

Today seniors are part of the fastest growing generation in history. Their numbers will double within the next twenty-five years. They also are living longer. Assisting older seniors in business, the community, and our families will become a common occurrence.

What I know from my many years of working with seniors is that human connection is the greatest gift you can give them. Technology is rapidly changing our lives, and it might make everyday tasks a little easier, but it will never replace human connection. Seniors thrive on human-to-human connection, yet loneliness is becoming an epidemic problem for older people.

The next time you connect with a senior, put yourself in their shoes. Show patience, respect, and kindness. You might be the only person they talk to that day, or even that week. That's why it's so important to enhance the quality of the moments you spend with them. Every interaction is an opportunity to make a difference in not only their lives, but also your own.

Collectively, by raising our awareness to the everyday challenges faced by many older adults, we can have a significant positive impact on their lives. Together we can create a senior-friendly world!

Lucky Lauridsen, RN, is an educator, speaker, and author. She is a heart-centered solutions provider that helps organizations create senior-friendly brands. As a champion for treating seniors right, she raises awareness to everyday challenges faced by many seniors, positioning companies to better serve and support them. She fosters winning situations for employers, employees, and seniors.

www.agewisebusiness.com

The Enemy Within: Ten Tips to Avoid Self-sabotage

Johnnie Lloyd

There is a voice and part of us that we cannot escape: the voice in our head that has the benefit of knowing our deepest fears and our greatest desires. That spot is where we make choices to be our best self or unleash destructive tendencies of self-sabotage.

Sabotage, according to the dictionary, means to deliberately damage, obstruct, wreck, or destroy. Self-sabotage creates problems and interferes in our lives, goals, vision, purpose, and success. Self-sabotage can include procrastination, drugs, alcohol, sex, overeating, and unhealthy emotional, physical, mental, and spiritual behaviors. This is not about excuses; this is about being self-aware. When you know better, you can do better— through the power of choice.

No matter how much we love people or ourselves, or think that our lives are perfectly balanced, anyone can do something to destroy everything through one act in a moment.

What's in us that would cause us to snap and do things that are diametrically opposed to our vision, goals, and dreams? What can cause us to sabotage ourselves the moment we are about to get what we've always wanted, prayed for, and fought for? We all know people who climbed the corporate ladder, lost the weight, got a fantastic opportunity, and then suddenly did something that caused everything to crumble.

All of us have habits we know are not good that open us to physical, emotional, professional, and spiritual sabotage. We can make it to the highest level in our organization, and then fear of others, fear of success, past issues, or our emotions cause us to do something to self-sabotage our win and we are left with a legacy of failure. That is not what any of us deserve; however, under all the money, power, brilliance, boldness, and bravery, our lack of self-control and self-awareness can sabotage everything and leave us in awe of what occurred. We may not think it is fair, but people tend to remember the last thing they saw in the media about us. People typically judge others by the last action or transaction they made. They judge us from a snapshot that just happened. So, with that in mind, how do brave, bold, brilliant women avoid self-sabotage? I'm glad you asked! Here are ten tips.

1. **Do not think you are exempt—kryptonite is real and destructive and will weaken all your superpowers**. Do not overlook people, places, or things that may be disruptive and or destructive. Being aware of what self-sabotage is and how you are triggered is priceless. Remember, knowing your strengths and weaknesses is not about fear—it is a power move.

2. **Keep something bigger in front of you and be the leader as you manage your power through how you use your time, money, and influence**. Even as your life shifts, keep moving forward by being the best version of yourself daily. You are not dead, so live a full and meaningful life. What that means to each of us is a choice.

3. **Look for power inside you—just as the rudder of a ship guides it, use your mouth and your beliefs to guide you**. "My guiding light is my belief in God." You may have other values or guiding principles. Just remember that you personally choose whatever principles and/or beliefs you are guided by. Do not overlook character and integrity; and most people hear what you say, but believe what you do. Let your actions speak louder than your words.

4. **Know your boundaries and stay true to who you are—limitless opportunities come when this key is properly utilized**. The development of strong boundaries acts as an invisible barrier, force field, or filter that regulates the flow from external forces, including people. Boundaries enforce your non-negotiables, and making the choice daily to enforce your established boundaries is an essential success skill.

5. **Teach others how to treat you and be authentic to who you are and your definite purpose**. It is imperative to figure out what matters to you beyond what you have been told or see in others' lives. Knowing your why will help drive, motivate, and encourage you to endure the journey I call the "Process of How."

6. **Stay teachable by being a river and not a reservoir. Reservoirs are artificial places were water is stored and can be dammed up to control**. A river is a natural body of water that promotes life and has a natural flow. So be encouraged to be like the water in a river that flows and impacts everything it touches.

7. Stay humble and loyal and give back. Communication is not only words of humility; it's the actions that back up your words that are what really speak to others the loudest. My mentor, John Maxwell, said it best: "Everybody communicates, but few connect." When you connect, your impact is felt, and transformation can occur. Know that you matter as you grow, pay it forward into programs, causes, and people.

8. Focus on leaving a legacy of "purpose." Know what you would like to be remembered for in your public, private, and professional life—especially in the social media-driven environment we live in today.

9. Run away from destruction, deception, and deceit. Speak the truth. Consider your values, stability, efficiency, productivity, compassion, mentorship, fellowship, and wisdom. You do not have to accept behaviors, language, actions, and disrespectful or invasive behaviors from others.

10. Our highest level of success is with others, so maintain a healthy life support system that offers opportunities for regular accountability, mentorship, and growth from a holistic perspective of spirit, soul, and body. "Checkup from the neck up" is important for mental, physical, spiritual, and emotional well-being.

Utilize these tips daily and be encouraged. Avoid self-sabotaging tendencies without excuses, not allowing your past to negate your future. Choose to take your control back and soar to greater heights with limitless possibilities. Find support as needed—you are not alone.

Johnnie Lloyd, chief visionary officer for JB Lloyd and Associates, LLC with virtual capability, specializes in transformational development. Johnnie is an international speaker, bestselling author, and financial guru servicing profit and nonprofit organizations. As a keynote or breakout session speaker, she provides insight for greater levels of productivity and profitability and supports transformation to next-level success.

www.johnnielloyd.com

Body Language

Renée Lucky

Youth is not a time of life—it is a state of mind. It is not a matter of ripe cheeks, red lips, and supple knees. It is a temper of the will, a quality of the imagination, a vigor of the emotions. It is freshness of the deep springs of life. Nobody grows old by merely living a number of years. People grow old by deserting their ideals. Years wrinkle the skin, but to give up enthusiasm wrinkles the soul.
SWAMI BUA, AGE 110

At age forty, my husband and I were blessed with the birth of our daughter. Although I continued to work a couple of hours per week, I was the main caregiver for the first five years of my daughter's life. When she entered grade one, I decided to increase my working hours.

My career in the fitness industry began at age sixteen. Teaching group fitness and personal training had been my main gigs. In my thirties, I competed in several natural bodybuilding shows. Sharing my passion for health and fitness has been my primary calling throughout my life.

I decided that teaching yoga classes seemed like the best choice for me. I could work early mornings, daytime, and evenings. This schedule would not interfere with school or child minding. Seeing lots of people every day and choreographing classes was just what I felt I needed. I was excited to teach all styles of yoga, but especially hot yoga, my favorite style to practice. The yoga studio that I had previously taught at welcomed me back with open arms. The studio had expanded to ten locations, so I could work at any of them.

Here I was at age forty-six, super stoked to be back teaching regular classes! I felt amazing! I was meeting people and sharing my enthusiasm for health and wellness on a daily basis. My body was lean and strong. I felt that I was setting a fantastic example for my young daughter. Life was amazing—or so I thought.

Although my intention was to return to teaching yoga, I accepted opportunities to teach fitness-style classes. The yoga studio had branched out and was offering sculpt, spin, Pilates, and TRX classes, among others. I even designed a core class which was offered throughout the company. I began teaching eleven to seventeen classes per week. I was exhausted but exhilarated at the same time.

My days were filled with getting up early, eating on the fly, consuming large amounts of caffeine, showering often, and getting to bed late. I escorted my daughter to and from school each weekday, and I volunteered a couple hours per week in her classroom. In essence, there was very little downtime for me to practice what I was teaching to my students. My personal self-care was now taking the back seat.

"Listen to your body." "Honor, accept and respect your current conditions." "Go at your own pace." These are words that I have spoken thousands of times. Although these phrases rang true to my heart, I allowed my mind to rationalize. I could see that our financial concerns were being remedied. I felt that I was making an impact on the world around me. I felt that I could do anything I put my mind to.

After about a year or so of this intense schedule, my foot began to develop a blister. I covered the affected area and continued to work, ignoring the pain and discomfort. As it worsened, I sought medical advice. The condition was misdiagnosed, and the pain worsened. With my foot blistered, cracking, and oozing, I went to a naturopathic clinic. After seeing two doctors there, the condition was properly diagnosed: It was a severe case of eczema. My body was extremely inflamed, and my adrenals were severely taxed. The doctor commented that I was pushing my body to the same limits as an Olympic athlete. I wasn't eating enough or resting enough to support the amount of activity I was doing.

Despite this humbling report, I continued to race through my days, teaching and giving 100-plus percent. And then one day I reached a crisis point. I was out walking with my family and had to stop because I couldn't breathe and felt extremely weak. We went to a walk-in medical clinic where the doctor diagnosed me with a severe case of strep throat and bronchitis.

I had no choice but to put a temporary halt to teaching. I was in pain and very sad. I could not taste food and had no desire to smile. My body was shutting down. I thought I was going to die.

I was in a position to reflect. My intentions had backfired. I thought that being away from home in the evenings would give my husband the opportunity to bond with our daughter. Even though that was indeed happening, my absence was taking away from our connection as a family. When we were together, I was often preparing for the following day's events or too tired to participate fully.

I finally accepted that my body was burned out. I made the decision to teach less. Very soon, I began to notice how much I had been pushing my body. My pace had been at a constantly high level, despite what was going on in my life. The energy required to "perform" each day was immense. I had to be physically, intellectually, and emotionally ready at all times. There was no room for a bad day. I was clearly not honoring, accepting, and respecting my current conditions.

Life has taught me well. Our most valuable commodity is our time and energy. We will age gracefully when we learn to honor, accept, respect, and love these amazing bodies that house our incredible spirits. Taking the time to rest and relax is the best gift we can give ourselves. This gift ultimately spills over to make the whole world a better place.

Namaste.

Renée Lucky was born and raised in Vancouver, BC, Canada. As a teenager she taught gymnastics and group fitness classes. After winning several titles as a competitive natural bodybuilder, Renee became a personal trainer and yoga instructor. Now, at age fifty-one, she plans to share her strategies for aging gracefully.

www.reneelucky.com

A Resilient Vision

Melani Luedtke-Taylor

I got my very first pair of glasses when I was five years old. I still remember standing on the low retaining wall that surrounded our backyard, wearing those tiny new Strawberry Shortcake-framed lenses. When I looked down, I couldn't figure out why the sidewalk seemed to be miles below my feet. No one had thought to tell me that my eyes needed time to adjust, so I pretended that I was teetering on top of a tall mountain. I jumped off, thinking I would never land. Imagine my surprise when my shoes touched the sidewalk just a second later, my body completely unscathed.

Even then, at some level I knew.

At age sixteen, I traveled with my mother, my brother, and my sister to Boston's Massachusetts Eye and Ear Hospital for tests. It was a miserable trip, full of doctors, seizures, yelling, fainting, and an accident that could have blinded me forty years prematurely. However, at the end, I went home bruised and scarred and with the confirmation that my brother and I had been inflicted with the eye disease that has plagued my father's family for generations.

Retinitis Pigmentosa, or RP, is a degenerative disease that affects the rods and cones in the retina and causes night and color blindness, tunnel vision, and even complete loss of sight. It is estimated that 100,000 people in the United States are affected with RP, all to varying degrees. There currently isn't a cure; however, there are some ideas on how to slow the progression.

Even though I was diagnosed with RP, I never noticed any other significant symptoms or had any noticeable issues until my early thirties. I seemed to be bumping into more stationary objects than before. There wasn't a chair, "wet floor" sign, or open cupboard that didn't see my knee, foot, shoulder, or head bump into its edge, but I quickly dismissed this as my perpetual clumsiness, for which I could receive an award.

Or so I thought.

It wasn't until my six-year-old daughter decided that she was angry and tried stalking off into a busy street that I had to admit that there might be something more I should start worrying about. I grabbed her just in time and pulled her back to the curb, but in doing so, I slammed my face into a parking meter, breaking my glasses and causing quite the jolt to my eye socket. When my eye started swelling, we went to the emergency room where, after giving my story, my husband had to answer a series of questions. These questions were obviously intended to understand if he, and not the parking meter, was the culprit.

After fifteen years, he hasn't quite forgiven me for that.

At the time, though, I was too busy worrying about the present to even think about the future. I was a marketing strategist for a Fortune 50 technology company, working on a new program. Some weeks I spent seventy or eighty hours holed up in my home office, attending meeting after meeting.

But life has a way of forcing us to recognize what we don't want to notice.

It was spring, in the middle of the week. My daughter was at school, and I was already on my eighth conference call of the day when I heard the front door open. My husband placed his keys on the glass table, as he always did when he got home. Today, however, he was hours too early.

I called out to him, asking why he was home. "I am on the way to the hospital for an emergency blood transfusion," he answered. "Are you coming?"

Knowing his sense of humor, I thought he was joking. He wasn't. In a flash, I packed up, and off we went. He had the transfusion, and all ended well, but I had completely missed all the signs of his illness. He had been incredibly tired, his mother had commented that he looked a little pale, and he was a little too soft-spoken. I had noticed none of it. We were told that day that he should have died. It was a miracle he was still with us.

People talk about their defining moment—the event that changed their perspective. That was mine.

I started drawing my own personal boundaries, figuring out what was truly important. It was now time to focus on what would happen if I lost my eyesight. For myself, for my husband, for our young daughter.

It wasn't easy having to come to terms with an uncertain future. I am a strong believer in changing what you can by fighting hard, but for a situation that you are unable to change, I believe that you can accept it and change your attitude instead.

Trust me, it was easier said than done. I went through the first four of the five stages of grief—denial, anger, bargaining, and depression—before acceptance even seemed possible. I railed against the change. I wanted options. I wanted safety. I wanted to be able to see my grandchildren grow up—something my grandfather never had the opportunity to do.

Honestly, it is still something I continually work on. There isn't a day that goes by that I am not frustrated because I can't see something on the floor to pick up, or I lose a bottle cap and can't find it, or I trip over the cat. Again. You would think the poor animal would have learned by now, right?

Then, one day, I realized that acceptance of an inevitable situation is not resignation. No, resignation implies that you wallow in the outcome. For me, that was not an option. Ever.

To prove that, I created a vision board and included all of the activities that I wanted to accomplish. This was meant to keep me on task and help me to remember what I still had left to achieve, regardless of the disease's progression.

One of the tasks on that board was to continue educating myself. My father had lost his job because of the disease and returned to school to become a teacher. I am very proud of him for that, but I didn't want to wait until my career ended to take the next step. Instead, I immediately went back to school and earned my bachelor's, master's, and multiple certifications. This was my way of being prepared for whatever the illness threw at me. I believed that education gave me more options. I was afraid that when my disease came to light, I would need something to combat the perception—not only of others, but also my own.

As for my career, I grew into a corporate conference manager. I was a master at hiding my disease, choosing not to share my challenges with my coworkers. Any tasks that were difficult, such as going behind the screen in the dark, navigating an expo floor during the build, or attending receptions after hours, I made sure to delegate to others.

The perception of others is something I thought about often. Would my co-workers treat me differently? Would they still think that I could perform my job? Would I still be highly considered for promotions? Perception. Is that something to fear? Do you think of someone differently once you realize they are battling something big? How people perceived me was the reason that I took unnecessary risks, pushing the boundaries of safety to be sure I wasn't found out.

It wasn't until years later that I finally had to let a few trusted friends in on my secret. It was pretty hard to explain away tripping over a cement bench in an otherwise empty hallway. I was very discriminating in whom I told, choosing to confide in people I felt wouldn't judge my ability to do my job based on my disease rather than my talent. The fear of people thinking differently of me was always present.

I was coping every day. I found myself memorizing everything so I didn't have to rely on my sight. At home, I knew exactly where I took my shoes off, how many steps from my bed to the bathroom, and how far the couch was from the front door. At work, I had to be sure how many chairs were in an aisle in a general session, how many rooms were on a floor of a conference center, and where the walking path from my hotel room to the staff room was.

It was beyond exhausting, but my memory and strong preparation were essential to coping with my eyesight gradually becoming worse.

That was just not sustainable, however. Being unable to see well and finding myself in a dark location or a busy street without directions or a loud, unknown space can be highly stressful. Panic attacks and anxiety became a common occurrence. I had to start becoming more accepting of calculated risks.

I once found myself in a dark, crowded bar in Dublin. My husband had gone to scout a location where we could sit so I stood near the band, listening until he came back for me. A few minutes went by before someone nearby started up a conversation with me. I was having a hard time hearing him with the band, and I definitely couldn't see him. When my husband returned, he politely told the gentleman that I wasn't going to return his "high-five" because I had no idea his hand was there in the first place. I laughed, apologized, and we left.

That story makes me laugh every time I think about it. It's embarrassing, sure. The reality is that people don't know that I can't see because I do not carry a cane (a perception issue that I am still working on overcoming). I have been called every name in the book, most completely inappropriate to share. I have had to stop worrying so much about what everyone else's perception is. I have had to stop being angry and hurt and just start combatting the negativity with positivity.

Robin Williams said, "Everyone you meet is fighting a battle you know nothing about. Be kind. Always."

I am not special. We all are dealing with hidden demons: a sick spouse or child, a parent who needs extra care, an impending divorce, or acclimating to a new city or country. Not all handicaps are apparent—whether they are physical or emotional. You never know what battle someone is fighting at home or behind their keyboard at work.

Today, I have 10 percent of my vision remaining. I have transitioned careers from a conference manager to a marketing, event, and personnel consultant so that I can work from my home. My husband and I have discussed the "hows" of our future life. How will we travel? How can I maintain my independence when I can't drive? How do we set up our home and life to make accommodations?

These are certainly discussions that no one looks forward to having, but they are entirely necessary.

I continually focus on acceptance and coping, but I refuse to sit idly by while my eyesight continues to diminish. I am on my second vision board, having crossed off everything that was on the first. And I worry far less about what people think about me.

I have promised myself that I will always be that kindergartner on that mountaintop. Even if I find myself bruised and scarred after jumping, I will continue to take those risks and push on. I will continue to work on accepting, preparing, and coping.

Because I believe I can. And I believe that no matter what challenge you might be facing, you can, too.

Melani Luedtke-Taylor is on a mission to encourage resilience through acceptance, preparation, and coping (#APC). She is a TEDx speaker, MBA graduate, certified coach, teacher, and marketing strategist, but as a wife, mother, and professional battling an impending disability, she focuses on creating new experiences while helping others realize their potential. Our world needs more empathy and less judgment as everyone is struggling with an invisible personal challenge. Visit her website and tell Melani your #APC story.

www.melaniltaylor.com

FROM FAILURE TO RECOVERY

Yvette McQueen, MD

I had finally made it. My high school dream was a reality. I was in medical school to be a doctor. And all was well.

That was me thirty-one years ago: naïve and thinking that life followed a straight line—that if you followed the rules you would get the outcome you expect. Well, I learned that life is not a straight line and failure provides the valleys needed to shine on the mountaintop.

I decided to become a doctor during tenth grade biology class; during twelfth grade advanced biology, my partner and I dissected a cat but sewed it back up. I followed the usual track for pre-med and biology majors, but I soon knew it was not for me. I have always had the urge to be different and not follow the direct path. I completed two years of college but left due to financial reasons and unfulfillment. I worked in a graphic arts store, where I learned commercial artist skills and explored my artistic side.

I returned to college after a year and a half, this time on my terms. I moved away from my hometown, supported myself financially, and explored several areas of learning. I graduated with a Physiology Bachelor of Science degree with a minor in Political Science. But I also took classes in acting, golf, behavioral psychology, and writing. Due to poor MCAT exam scores, I did not go to medical school immediately after college. I worked in research for two years and was finally accepted to medical school.

I was joyous, ecstatic, and living my dream. But I let love and life get in my way. I put too much focus in an unhealthy relationship and fell into financial despair. These circumstances led to a depressive state and I neglected my studies. Through my faith in God, encouragement from friends, and the love of my family, I pulled myself out of the hole, got a job, and attempted to complete my first year of medical school. But it was too late. I failed three out of four classes. The curriculum committee separated me from medical school; and despite appeals, I was not allowed to return and repeat classes typically granted for the first-year courses.

I returned home embarrassed and deflated. My family was understanding and supportive, but also forthright about me getting my life together. I had a foundation from parents that said "When life knocks you down, pull yourself back up and face adversity. There's always an alternate road." And that's what I did. I also had my spiritual foundation. My belief told me that God has a plan even though he hadn't shared it with me. God places us in positions at a specific time in life and intersects us with people for a purpose. I knew I would be a doctor but not at that time.

I worked as a substitute high school teacher, and through a temporary agency, I got a job as a secretary and personal assistant. One of my assignments was at the local medical school, working with a female cardiologist. After a month of doing her manuscripts, grants, and chapters, she inquired about my background. I gave her my honest story. She hired me immediately as her research assistant and encouraged me to set a goal to return to medical school. During the three years I worked for her, I completed several research protocols for cardiology advancement and attended many of the medical school classes. After a petition to my original medical school, by God's grace I returned to medical school.

I was humbled but determined. I knew I could not succeed alone. I knew I needed to seek support and help. I had learned to tell my story, not be reclusive, and YELL when I needed help. I had matured and now understood the politics; I had gained networking skills, knew how to seek funds, and learned the components of success.

They now call me DOCTOR.

I learned that I might fail at a task at a certain time, but I was not a failure. And that would not be my last failure. Failure is a learning process and a step toward success. Failures are sprinkled throughout life. It's how you react to the failures that determines your forward progress, or what some people call success.

So, once you have failed, learned, and grown from your mistakes, accepted yourself as "you," and learned to depend on others for help, put all your energy into actions to move past the failure. I call these recovery steps "Rules of Engagement" to success.

1. Take action. Paralysis is nonproductive; move forward after acceptance and analyzing your failure.

2. Have a positive mindset, believe in yourself, and know that perfection is a myth. Use daily affirmations to maintain positivity.
3. Build a community. You cannot do this alone, so abandon the "I" hanging out by itself. Surround yourself with positive like-minded, and successful people. A community is needed for support, guidance, mentorship, and empathy.
4. Set multiple small goals that are achievable and realistic.
5. Be flexible and adaptable. Learn to transition into another season. Adjust to the circumstances and overcome the obstacles thrown in your pathway to success.
6. Eliminate negativity around you; don't allow others to take away your joy.
7. Practice self-care. Be kind to yourself. Know your physical and mental limitations and know when to rest. It takes energy and stamina to achieve your goals.

FAILURE is Faithful Acts In Life U Rebound Enthusiastically
Fail fast, fail forward, and fail forgivably toward recovery.

Success is not final; failure is not fatal: it is the courage to continue that counts.
WINSTON CHURCHILL

Yvette McQueen, MD, is a global physician on a mission to educate about health, travel wellness, and disease prevention. She is an Emergency Medicine physician and Travel Doctor. Dr. McQueen offers a lifestyle modifications course, and she is an international travel group physician. She is also a speaker, author, consultant, and provides international medical teaching.

www.yvettemcqueenmd.com

Reclaiming Our Power, Reclaiming Our Voice, Reclaiming Our Choice

Lakichay Nadira Muhammad

One of my beloved ancestors once made a powerful statement that I will never forget: "The hospital is not a place for a pregnant women; it is a place for those that are sick, and pregnancy is not an illness." Years later I was reminded of those words when I was blessed to witness a midwife-attended home birth. It was one of the most beautiful things I had ever seen. I knew that if God ever granted me the opportunity to be with child, I would want to re-create that same kind of magic.

By God's mercy and grace, a few years later I was blessed with the seed of life. I originally began my birthing journey aided and assisted by a wonderful and experienced midwife. But as fate would have it, I would make a decision early in my pregnancy to have a DIY birth. I knew that I wanted to experience what many of my ancestors experienced, and a healthy home birth was what I desired. Although I had no formal experience—which naturally caused a little fear to creep in—what I did have was great examples and the faith that I could deliver this gift with God's assistance.

For the next several months, I studied every book I could find relating to midwifery and natural childbirth until I became one with the knowledge I was blessed to discover. In addition, I began to tap into the energy and spirit of all the great and courageous women that had gone before me. I had so many examples from many of my ancestors who had served as midwives and delivered multiple babies with no formal training to the many women around the world who had been doing this since the beginning of time.

I prided myself on being the female version of God (some may say Goddess) and knowing that I could do anything that I put my mind to. On June 14, 2000, my thoughts became flesh and I was able to see my vision manifest in the person of my firstborn son. Three years later I was blessed to repeat this magical occurrence with the birth of my second son.

The birthing process, by far, is one of the most fulfilling and rewarding experiences that I've been blessed with. In truth, I believe that it is the closest any human being will ever come to God, because it is during these times that we must tap into our Godlike attributes. God must be present with us, guiding us every step of the way—how else does one explain such a beautiful and phenomenal experience? If you happen to be one of the many who have had this highly sacred opportunity, then you are more divinely connected than you may ever know. BIRTHING is so powerful that the entire experience should always be honored, reverenced, and highly regarded as one of the most sacred sacrifices known to man.

For the past two hundred-plus years, women in America have experienced a major shift as it relates to childbirth and the overall value of maternal health. This holistic art form that once was facilitated and assisted by skilled and experienced midwives was hijacked and corrupted by a male-dominated profession that was foreign to the art of child birthing. Healthy babies being born in the comfort of our homes slowly became a thing of the past, while hospital births attended by doctors and nurses began to be marketed and glorified as the "new and improved" way to give birth.

What happened? Who decided that this was best for women—and why? The truth of the matter is that birthing became a business! No longer honored and respected as a sacred experience influenced by nature, childbirth became an opportunity for the medical profession to create an additional means of income. An art form that is a natural life occurrence slowly began to be treated as a life-threatening illness that required the attention of so-called medical "experts."

Sadly, many nurses and doctors bought into the notion that women no longer deserved to have control over their maternal health. The freedom for a woman to choose how she gave birth was no longer an option, and home births and midwifery-attended births were ridiculed and looked down upon. Fear tactics scared women into thinking they were no longer safe in their homes. If they chose to have a midwife assist them in their birthing experience, somehow their babies would not get the "expert" care they needed.

Having a say in how a woman should birth her children is a God-given right. All women are born with a natural instinct to birth our babies. My experience gave me the strength to trust in myself and have the faith that ultimately afforded me the freedom to experience a God-assisted birth.

When it comes to a sacred decision centered around your birthing experience, no one should make the decision for you. Unfortunately, money and power have created a monopoly on the business of birthing. The cost to give birth in a hospital can average anywhere from $25,000 to $60,000. I am happy to say that my births were nearly 100 percent below cost.

My story is not meant to convince you about the type of birth you should have. I am here simply as an advocate for a woman's right to choose her birthing narrative without the influence or force of a history and a profession that has not always been kind or truthful regarding our maternal health, nor has always shown respect or valued the woman's divine power, sacred voice and God-given right to choose. I want to serve as an example and encourage mothers to gain more knowledge about our indigenous birthing traditions and maternal health practices around the world.

Remember, pregnancy is not an illness to be "treated"—instead, it is a natural gift from God to carry the seed of life, and it requires nurturing and care driven by love. You have options, and the role you play in your maternal health is extremely important and valuable!

Affectionately known as "The Queen of Self Improvement," Lakichay Nadira Muhammad is a wholistic health practitioner and mental health therapist. As a speaker, maternal health and parent advocate, womb wellness savant, and indigenous baby catcher, she believes that every woman is uniquely endowed with her own special gift, just waiting to be unwrapped.

www.thecenterforselfimprovement.com

THE ART AND SOUL OF OVERCOMING

Lisa Jean Nielson

I love my body, but for most of my life I hated it.

One of my first memories of self-destruction was when I was eight years old. Bending over the toilet, I forced my index and middle fingers down my throat in an attempt to produce evidence that I was sick enough to stay home from school. My desire to distance myself from any social situation where I could be called "big girl" or "huge" had become so great, I would do anything, even if it meant isolation.

Yet all I ever wanted was to be loved, to belong.

Fast-forward to my college years when my insatiable drive for perfection and achievement resulted in a list of accomplishments, including modeling contracts, beauty pageants, and theatrical opportunities. Yet no esteemed list could hide the all-consuming reality of a rampant eating disorder with no end in sight. After ten years of bulimia and anorexia, I was exhausted. I spent countless hours comparing my body with the images of models in magazines and wondering why, at nearly six feet tall, I hadn't been blessed with long, lean limbs. During this time, I often had grand images of cutting away fat and muscle and found myself even slicing into my own skin to relieve my anxiety.

Although I maintained good grades, a full schedule, and a polished appearance, my usual pattern was to starve myself for days at a time, which would inevitably result in binging and purging. These purges would involve self-induced vomiting or swallowing ever increasing amounts of laxatives and diuretics in combination to effectively rid my body of the food that I feared would cause weight gain. A great deal of strategy was required as I planned these managed binges, and I would often find myself too weak to stand, my body broken from full days of violent cramping and constant trips to the bathroom.

The peak of my self-destruction occurred when I was living on the eleventh floor of my college dorm. One particular winter weekend I found myself barely conscious on the dorm's communal bathroom floor. I was lying face down on the ice-cold white tile floor, no sound aside from the dripping of the sink faucet above me. My breathing was shallow and slow, and I felt myself fading away.

I managed to shift my aching body so I was lying on my side. "Who will find me?" I wondered. What was normally a busy and social floor full of friendly and diverse students was like a ghost town as many had gone home for the holiday break. I was alone.

I was sure my electrolytes were dangerously out of balance. The experience of being hospitalized so many times before had given me an awareness, a baseline to know when I had "gone too far." I was too weak to make a sound and my heart was beating slower and slower. The combination of diuretics and laxatives can be lethal, inflicting consequential effects on the heart and other organs.

"Please don't let me die!" I cried out to God, pleading for help to find my way back to my room, to my bed—where I would sleep for ten continuous hours and eventually regain my strength. I told no one of that day, allowing my shame to thrive once again in isolation.

Majoring in social work, I believed my purpose was found in helping. Even though it seemed impossible for me to accept grace and mercy for myself, there was comfort in seeing the progress of others. I took a field-related job working graveyard shifts at a behavioral group home for the disabled. Often when my work duties were complete, I would find myself alone in the quiet. I would lose myself in my sketchbook, finding solace and release as I poured out my hurt and rage in my drawings.

I had never taken any pride in my creativity, whether it was writing, singing, art, or theater, and was the first to downplay my efforts. My breakthrough came when, during a visit home, I reluctantly shared my drawings with my talented artist father. His reaction was warm and kind, and he encouraged me to keep developing as an artist and to allow whatever I was feeling to flow through. I began to understand that he had been dealing with grief, loss, and trauma all along through his own art. And though I would never know his level of talent in this arena, I could turn to art and creativity as a conscious choice in moments when I would normally choose self-destructive behavior. That day I finally knew I could replace my sick behaviors if I would allow it—and I had to allow it if I was to survive.

Around this time, I soon discovered my passion for makeup and building confidence in the faces I touched, and I spent hours practicing on myself and others. Sketching eyes, brows, and lips, I began to appreciate the beauty in each unique face. I finally felt alive in seeing how my makeup work positively impacted those I served, and this gave me the greatest sense of purpose!

Although my eating disorder still "hung around," I began to replace moments of upset, loneliness, or anxiety with creativity. The more I did so, the more of a new habit I developed. Sometimes what I created was raw and messy, rough and graphic, scary and abstract, but it moved emotion through and away from me, allowing for a full range of emotions and my rawest truths. We are all the summary and collection of experiences, both good and bad, which can be shared to touch and inspire others in beautiful and constructive ways.

The Art and Soul Movement is a call to arms for women and men of all ages to awaken and discover creativity and artistic expression, allowing for a shift in difficult moments of choice. This shift can act as a replacement for disordered eating, self-harm, substance abuse, and even suicide. This will be my life's work—it's not just for a season. Never in my life have I been more aware of the war and destruction declared on the soul than I am now. And never in my life have I been more committed to sharing this message of hope!

Lisa Jean Nielson is the founder of Art And Soul Girls, a movement of ritualistic self-compassion through creativity, service, and artistic expression. Lisa is a licensed esthetician and makeup artist with over twenty years of experience and is also a confidence coach and speaker.

www.artandsoulgirls.com

WALKING ALONE IN DARKNESS

Cheryl Peltekis, RN

I was starting to get frustrated. I wasn't sure if being frustrated felt better than being afraid. I couldn't see anything. I thought about giving up. I inched forward slowly. I felt sick to my stomach, and I was starting to shake. I could hear sounds from the cave. Owls, crickets, and maybe frogs. All I could do was think. I was alone in the pitch dark, and I had no clue what the next few moments were going to deliver to me. It's amazing to me, but times like this make us either panic or make us focus. In my mind I made the conscious decision to survive. I knew that if I could recall times when I faced my fears and came out of the experience stronger, I would be able to get through this horrible ordeal.

Suddenly the feeling of being a senior in high school came to my mind. I remembered getting ready to graduate and go to college and wishing I had a magic ball that could show me if the decisions I was making were correct. As I reflected on this memory, I reached with my hands as far as I could to feel for something, and I found large wet leaves on my left side. Good! At least if I keep walking while I was touching the leaves, I would be moving in one direction, which would hopefully lead me to safety.

Again, my mind wandered, and I thought about when I was done with college and had become an RN. I decided to open a business. It was probably one of the scariest things I ever did—risking my home to start a business at the age of twenty-six. I conquered the fear that new entrepreneurs face every day, and now I could get through this too.

Suddenly panic coursed through my body. For a moment, I felt sand at my feet and thought that maybe I was heading into an area of water. What could I be walking into? I kept moving, cheering myself on. I couldn't turn back now. I was too far into the darkness. I felt cool water at my feet. Where was I? Was I walking into deep water? I wished I could see where I was going. I kept going, and my mind did too.

I was back in 1993, and I was pregnant. I had read everything I possibly could to help me have a healthy pregnancy. I read every book I could about parenting and child development in the first year. I got my maternity nursing manual out and reviewed all the labor and delivery lessons. I felt like I was trying to get my Girl Scout badge, following the motto "always be prepared." But nothing could have prepared me for the experience of childbirth. As I reflected on that, suddenly I no longer felt water at my feet. The ground began to grow cold. I got the feeling that the cave was growing smaller. I thought I heard growling, and I pleaded out loud to get somewhere safe.

My mind went back to childbirth, and I began telling myself out loud . . . I may have even screamed . . . "Push through! Do not give up!" I felt tears running down my face, and I began to tremble. I told myself, "You can do this!" I kept going, slowly and steadily into the darkness, and I told myself, *I am not going to freeze to death. I am not going to die.* I was once again on the delivery table. The doctor told me to push, and with one last push, this beautiful baby girl was in the doctor's arms, with a wonderful sound of crying. Suddenly, I was brought back to my truth.

I thought I heard something. It sounded like someone was walking close to me. I held my breath so I could really focus on any sounds. I was so scared! The tears returned on my checks, and I desperately wanted to be anywhere but there. I didn't move as I continued to listen.

My awareness left reality once again, and I was brought to a place of peace in my mind. I was admiring my children. Eleni now twenty-six, a clinical psychologist. Nicolette now twenty-five, and an RN. Tommy, my only son, now twenty-two and just months from graduating college. Alexandra, my Peanut, a freshman in college with a 3.9 GPA for her first semester. My baby girl Angela, just about to turn eighteen and excited about attending college in the fall. My life had given me great adventures and had been full of incredible love and kindness. I had all that I ever needed and more. I did things my way, and I had been so blessed. I had to get out of this situation. They were all waiting for me. I picked up my pace in the darkness with confidence. I didn't feel afraid anymore. I knew I was going to survive!

Finally, I saw light in the distance. I had made it! I had faced my fear of being all alone in complete darkness. I made it through the Xenses Park in Mexico—a thirty-minute walk in complete blackness in a tunnel. Seven people go in, and usually only two complete the journey. Many give up. I used previous successes to push on. This experience made me realize the strategy I had used throughout my whole life: recalling past accomplishments to help me push on to new levels of success.

This is what I want to share this with you; I want you to use this tool for yourself. No matter how small the accomplishment, you went from crawling to walking; you learned how to read and ride a bike. Use those past successes to push through and help you reach levels of incredible success. Face your fears—I promise you, it is liberating. Share this tactic whenever you see someone struggling. Remind them of what they have overcome in the past so they, too, can push through.

Cheryl Peltekis, RN, is an infectious leader in the home health and hospice industry as well as the mother of five children. A bestselling author, she has been seen on TV shows and stages around the world. Cheryl's nickname is "The Solutionist"—and she knows how to lead a winning team!

www.homecaresales.com

MIND YOUR BRAIN,
MIND YOUR STORY

Jill Perla

Pay attention. Not to me, silly, but to you. Yes, you. Can you hear it? Can you hear that little voice inside? What's going on in that beautiful mind of yours? I urge you to turn up the volume and start listening to your inner voice. If you tune in, I guarantee your life will be much fuller and happier! If you think your life is riddled with hardship, I urge you to reframe your thoughts and see how small shifts in your thinking can help. Let's explore how I did it.

Growing up with five siblings, including a sister who was hard of hearing and aphasic, came with challenges. My sister is smart; don't get me wrong. But you see, messages would get botched inside her brain. Years ago professionals told my parents not to learn sign language, so communicating with her was dicey at best. I found myself to be the TV show interpreter (no closed-captioning back then). There was resentment growing up, but now I realize that through helping her, I learned patience and am an excellent communicator today. See? A creative win for me.

Society sees any disease of the brain as shameful. It's ridiculous. I do believe society is shifting a bit, though. My mom is bi-polar and has struggled with depression for years. I remember coming home from school, and she would be "sick." I never understood why as a child, and it took me years to understand that her brain had a chemical imbalance. But from this I learned empathy, and I thank God all the time that I do not suffer from this.

As a child, I learned coping skills. The number one skill was to shut out pain—just keep running forward, don't look back. Do anything you can to be the peacemaker. Many decisions I have made in life were based on not hurting anyone's feelings and making sure I didn't shine too brightly. I had to keep a lid on my true self so much so that I developed what my mom called the six-month breakdown. I stuffed my feelings so much so that I would faint. I passed out in church, while on a horse, on a city sidewalk, on a subway—you name it, I've passed out. The feelings I had inside were so buried they had to come out some way, and that is how I coped.

Not stopping to listen to what my inner voice was telling me, I just plowed through life. I loved making money, much like my successful father. I was good at it, but I knew there was something missing and could not put my finger on it. Throughout my life I was the peacemaker. I actually thought I could manage other people's feelings. I am an empath and intuitive, so it was easy, especially since I didn't have to look at my feelings. If you aren't tuned into what your needs are, though, the help you give will ring hollow.

In my forties, my father suffered with dementia. Having been a Harvard grad, this seemed even more of a blow. During his therapies, he created art, and from this I learned the love of painting. He has since passed away from this devastating disease, but I took up painting and have a thriving, self-sustaining, and profitable business.

The art was one step closer to sharing my truth. But I hid behind my art. I still did not let anyone know who I was because I was afraid. It was easier to hustle and run.

Turning up the voice inside of me has made me realize that I may be able to help others who suffer in silence. Now I realize that creative minds are just as important as analytical minds. It took me years to believe that I, too, am just as smart as my super successful book-smart siblings.

From my journey of helping with a sibling with aphasia, my mother with bi-polar disorder, and my father with dementia, I have learned a few things. I had to be creative in all aspects of my life. When you are met with adversity, small or big, you have to think creatively! Even when my husband was deployed to Iraq twice, once during the birth of my second daughter, I had to dig deep—much like I am now that my husband is facing cancer.

It has taken me years to push aside ego and stop running from my truth. I am here today to tell you to stop. Stop running from your story. Share your story so that others can learn. Don't shut your story out of your journey. Your story is what makes you special. I know it sounds cliché, but take it from me: I went full-tilt ahead and tried to bury my story by hiding behind my achievements in business and the accolades from my art awards.

Through my journey, I have seen how brains that aren't quite right can be beautiful, frustrating, special, magical, and downright terrible all at the same time. But when you open your own eyes to the story that shapes you, your business, your personal life, everything—the veil lifts and a light shines, and boy, what a wonderful feeling it is! It is how you interpret it to yourself and others that decides whether or not you are going to be a forward-thinking winner.

*Internationally collected, award-winning artist, former vice president of finance, former manager of a large scientific meeting, experienced high-tech sales executive, board member, and vice president of a networking organization, **Jill Perla** brings a unique perspective and shows how to have creative wins in all aspects of life.*

www.jillperlaart.com

Unleash Your Most Powerful and Authentic Self

Michela Quilici

There are hundreds of people in the auditorium. I'm about to do my flamenco dance as the title character in the show. Nervous is too mild a word to describe how I feel. Electric anxiety is running through my body as I stand on stage in my opening pose. Just before curtain call, the voices of judgment, shame, and belittlement echo in my mind. I am plagued with a deep insecurity that I'm not good enough and that I don't belong on stage. This is the inner dialogue that I battle.

I was raised in a traditional Italian home, and my father could blow a fuse quite easily when he disapproved of something—like when I spoke in English and he bellowed out, "*Parla in Italiano!* (Speak Italian!)" Because of this, my mother constantly walked on eggshells and taught my sister and I to *never upset your father.*

Or when I was six years old, sitting at the dinner table with my parents, and I asked a question that seemed to challenge my father's opinion. My mother kicked me under the table and said, "*Basta!* (Enough!)"

I've lost count of the number of times I got kicked in the shins and was told to be quiet. I remember thinking that it was dangerous to talk. Every time I spoke, my words seemed to be met with anger and rage. Eventually, I developed a debilitating fear of speaking and a terrible stutter. I closed myself off and began cowering in shame. I was so shut down due to trauma and emotional abuse that I was sure I would be destined to spend my adult life hiding from the world.

Do you ever feel like you need to hide parts of yourself because you think people won't accept you for who you are?

I know at a visceral level what it's like to not be seen or heard, and to be misunderstood. I've been on a lifelong journey to reclaim my voice—and use it to influence the perception of how I see myself and how others see me. Because when your voice isn't being heard, you're not able to make the impact you desire.

And that's why I do what I do.

So, how does a shy, introverted, sensitive child with a speech impediment and extreme performance anxiety become a public speaker and successful businesswoman?

Sometimes it feels like it's too risky to take a leap of faith and say yes to something new. But, as author Anais Nin says, "The day came when the risk to remain tight in a bud was more painful than the risk it took to blossom."

I have discovered three keys that will inspire you to unleash your most powerful and authentic self so you can navigate your business and your life, on purpose. I call them the Trifecta of Change.

1. Have Courage and Give Yourself Permission to Blossom. First, you must choose to give yourself permission to grow.

When I was eighteen years old, I had a college instructor who taught a class in professional sales. As I stuttered miserably during my oral exam, his aqua-blue eyes pierced me with kindness, and he said, "Your stutter will be your superpower, because you are being genuine, and people will trust you because of it."

He shifted my perspective about my disability from being a negative attribute holding me back to a positive catalyst that could propel me forward. Something about that encounter was very powerful for me. It motivated me to say, "Enough is enough! *Basta!*" It was time to take charge. First, I chose to reframe my disability, and second, I chose to get help from a speech therapist. With single-minded devotion, I worked with that therapist for almost a decade on the mechanics of speech fluency and the mindset work of dismantling old belief systems. The more I worked on my own personal development, the less I stuttered.

2. Reframe What's Holding You Back into a Catalyst That Propels You Forward. What IF . . . your biggest wound is actually your greatest gift in disguise? This is an opportunity to turn your history into the miracle that you are. And you CAN, but you have to be HUNGRY for it.

I wanted to be an effective dynamic speaker and as such, I cast a vision for myself that I would be somebody who didn't stutter. It's amazing what happens when you set an intention for what you want.

One rainy Wednesday evening, I walked into a Spanish bistro in North

Vancouver. It turned out that we would be entertained by a Flamenco dance group. As the Spanish dancer approached the dance floor, I felt the confidence emanating from her body. She started to dance, and something woke up inside of me. This woman was commanding the room with her power and her presence, and I wanted to be like her.

Have you ever experienced something that is so inspiring that it ignites you into action?

Seeing her mirror this possibility for me gave me permission to do it for myself. My hunger and desire became greater than my fear.

3) Get Crystal Clear about What You Want and Have the Conviction to Go After It. If you are brutally honest with yourself, what is it that you TRULY want?

Get CLEAR about what you want. Then GO GET IT!

The ONE thing that matters when you want to create change is YOU.

It's not about being good enough, smart enough, or prepared enough. It's about having the courage, confidence, and conviction to show up, speak up, and stand up.

Your future is not yet written.

There's an open page—and an empty stage—waiting for you.

It's your time to be seen and be heard.

Michela Quilici is a business navigator, award-winning business growth coach and marketing strategist, speaker, bestselling author, Forbes Coaches Council member, and creator and host of the Q Your Business Success podcast. She works with CEOs and business owners so they can get noticed, get clients, and get profitable using strategy, systems, and self-leadership.

www.michelaquilici.com

No Girl Left Behind

Vivien Rayam

When I think of my four-year-old daughter and her zest for life, I want her to know that she can be anything from a scientist to a computer programmer. A booming computer science industry, and our family's desire to create a lasting legacy led us to join the Code Ninjas franchise. It allows us a vehicle to promote STEM to the community through a program where kids learn to code, build a tribe, and develop critical thinking and problem-solving skills in a fun and interactive way. We even developed a girls STEM group at our Code Ninjas center in order to expose young girls in the community to careers in STEM. We have women in various roles speak with the girls, discuss confidence, and participate in hands-on projects.

In China some kids are being introduced to coding in preschool, and in the UK, coding is being taught to kids as early as age five. When you think about kids competing globally, developing STEM skills, especially in areas such as coding, will be necessary as the use of machine learning, augmented reality, and artificial intelligence will be commonplace in their adulthood.

Most young girls when asked what they want to be when they grow up say a teacher, doctor, veterinarian, lawyer, or nurse according to a poll by Gallop (2005).[1] These are all respectable professions. I wanted to be Oprah. However, there is a lack of interest in careers in Science, Technology, Engineering, and Math (STEM). The STEM sector is growing rapidly. A STEM survey by Emerson, a Missouri-based technology and engineering company, says the STEM worker shortage is at crisis levels in the US and more people are needed to fill these types of careers.[2] There are more jobs in the STEM industry than any other industry, and it is important for today's youth—especially young girls—to consider a career in this field. At our center, we have girls who want to be engineers, game developers, astronauts, and cyber security experts. Through Code Ninjas, we get to create avenues for them to explore their interests.

Career aspirations based on individual skills, curiosities, and beliefs are formulated during adolescence and shape the career choices that lead to a STEM career (Eccles, Vida, & Barber, 2004; Wang, 2012). I remember the awful computer class I had in high school and how boring it was, and most of the girls felt the same way. Parents, teachers, and mentors have the unique opportunity to expose young girls to careers they may not have considered because they never tried to develop those skills. A survey commissioned by Microsoft[3] of 11,500 girls across twelve European countries found that young girls in Europe became interested in STEM subjects around the age of eleven. However, by the time they turn fifteen, they lose interest due to gender and social expectations. Girls' self-confidence tends to drop in their teen years when issues of self-worth and body image become a priority.

From the pictures in magazines to motion pictures, often STEM-related roles are given to men. Representation is important because seeing someone who looks like you in a role subconsciously lets you know it is possible to attain it. Stereotypical roles of women as motivated by love and passion, weaker than men, and sexualized—especially in the current reality television culture—are some of the challenges with media representation. Ensuring that young girls stay engaged is important as they move from preteen to teenager. Some effective engagement strategies to keep girls interested in STEM include mentors, clubs or programs, and ongoing hands-on projects. Clubs or programs where STEM topics are covered in a way that stimulates a young girl's creativity, provides a safe place to grow, and builds their confidence are invaluable.

STEM careers can have a bad connotation for girls, so involving them in projects where they can problem solve, use logic, and think critically helps to nurture their interest in STEM. The Microsoft study also found that girls are more likely to pursue a career in this area if they think men and women will be treated equally in the workforce. Six in ten girls admitted they would feel more confident pursuing a STEM career if they knew men and women were already equally employed in these fields (Microsoft, 2017).

Overall, women are underrepresented across STEM careers, especially in engineering (14 percent), computer (25 percent), and physical science (39 percent) occupations, according to a 2018 study by Pew Research Center.[4] Even when women enter these fields, the retention rate is low for keeping them in the field. However, women are making some headway in some areas of STEM. As a matter of fact, women make up three-quarters of health care practitioners and technicians, the largest occupational cluster classified as STEM, with 9.0 million workers—6.7 million of whom are women (Pew Research Center, 2018).

What does this mean for our young girls? It is good news that some steps are being taken in the right direction. However, there is more work to be done. As our young girls prepare for jobs in the twenty-first century, skills such as coding will arguably be just as important as learning grammar.

I want girls to realize that careers in STEM are an option for them. Technology that will be created and implemented over the next few decades has to include the thinking skills of women, or the products and programs developed could miss out on the logic that is found in a female mind. Young girls will grow into tomorrow's problem solvers, inventors, and entrepreneurs. If they have the mindset that their options are limited, they could close the door on their best opportunities. However, when they have a growth mindset that focuses on a life of possibility, they are limitless.

1. https://news.gallup.com/poll/8371/Teen-Career-Picks-More-Things-Change.aspx.
2. https://www.emerson.com/en-us/about-us/emerson-and-stem.
3. https://money.cnn.com/2017/02/28/technology/girls-math-science-engineering/index.html.
4. https://www.pewresearch.org/fact-tank/2018/01/09/7-facts-about-the-stem-workforce/.

Vivien Rayam is the general manager and co-owner of Code Ninjas Snellville in Georgia. She works with youth to help them develop a love of computer programming and foster an interest in STEM careers. Her mission is to share the path of STEM as a viable option for all kids.

www.vivienrayam.com

A CONFIDENT STARE

Jeannine Rivers

I can remember it like it was yesterday: staring at my computer while working a nine-to-five job that was simply a necessity and definitely not the career of my dreams.

I was a bank manager, and every day I encountered people pursuing their dreams. I helped clients launch their business ventures. I helped them get loans, save money, and manage their finances for future travels abroad. As the years passed, I would watch my clients soar, live out one dream, and tackle new dreams.

Every day, I would rise to the occasion, put on my banking attire, and go to work. I was thriving. Promotion after promotion, I moved from personal banker to commercial banker and finally to branch manager. I managed twelve vibrant employees, and I was very good at helping them advance to new careers, encouraging them to rise to the next level of their dreams.

All the while, I myself was stuck behind a desk, wishing I was one of my clients. What I loved the most about my clients and employees was their ability to realize that they had the power to fulfill their destiny. Yet I couldn't begin to figure out how to get where they were; I lacked the ability to see the first step needed to accomplish even one of my dreams.

For twenty years I sat at my desk—unhappy, restless, and frustrated. But there were also times that I would confidently stare at my computer, which represented every loan file, bank account, and customer I had ever assisted. I would literally talk to the computer. In a fierce and determined voice, I would say, "I won't do this forever. One day I will live my dream and be happy!" I was confident that my computer was listening to my every word and received my confident stare as a warning of my departure.

A confident stare is the ability to physically look at an obstacle in your life with keen eyes and then find the fortitude to attack the obstacle without allowing it to leave you feeling uneasy, restless, and unhappy. A confident stare allows you to grab hold of the obstacle and look it directly in the eye, all while deciphering it and figuring out the best way to manage it so the result is a winning situation. A confident stare means you are determined not to allow the obstacle to define you, mold you, nor allow you to stay stuck on a road to nowhere.

There is no question that sometimes the steps needed to accomplish your dreams are automatically mapped out for you. You won't always have to put in the work because a part of your destiny has already been designed for you.

During my time as a bank manager, my daughter was a small child. I thought living my life as a starving musician and becoming an entrepreneur was out of the question. Nonetheless, I knew one day it would happen. I didn't understand how, but I knew it was just a matter of when. Yet not all dreams automatically come true. Sometimes faith is not enough, and you must learn how to put in the work.

I have learned from my own life that unhappiness, dismay, and confusion can lead to making poor decisions, ones that can, and will, affect the outcome of our dreams. Detours in life can serve as lessons and give us the skills needed to accomplish our dreams. You may know what your destiny is, yet you will still need to plan.

When I look back at my time in the banking industry, it seemed that all I had was a confident stare, a computer, and some powerful words. I didn't have a physical plan written down on paper; all I had was faith and a feeling. I eventually learned that my faith was not enough and that I also needed to put in some hard work to accomplish my dreams.

My life has afforded me many opportunities to learn that I had the same authority within myself as my former clients and employees did. I had the privilege to utilize my energy and power to do better in my life when I knew I was off track. I learned to put in the work, and along the way I developed a skill set that propelled me forward.

The phrase *a confident stare* is more than just a notion; it requires action. It's what happens during the process that is so powerful. For me, a confident stare is both an elimination station and a birthing station. It's where I mentally cast out doubt, fear, and feelings of inadequacy. I silence the negative voices and deaden the negative energy. My confident stare turns into a vision that in time reenergizes my very being. My doubt turns into certainty, fear is transformed into confidence, and feelings of inadequacy are replaced by the knowledge of my strongest points. The negative voices are now drowned out by the soaring of my own voice reassuring myself of my tenacity. A voice of will, to get up and DO!

Many of you might say that a confident stare is the same as meditation, an act of prayer or the action of mapping out a plan on paper. This may be true for many of you. But not for me!

Often, as I now sit in my home office, I get lost staring at my computer. I confidently stare into my future, and this is what I see: my vision for women and girls in this world and how I will nurture them, lift them up, and help them move to what's next in their lives. I literally touch, hug, and hold them in my heart and soul. I see and feel their struggles and then form a concrete plan for them that is viable and easy to grab on to.

I also see myself and my own personal goals. I see the power of the process and the changes I will make within my own life's journey.

In this season of your life, I hope you will allow the power of your own confident stare to move you into what's next for you too.

Jeannine Rivers is an author, motivator, and musician who enjoys inspiring people with her heartfelt stories, life lessons, and music of hope. As an inspirational speaker and confidence coach, she facilitates workshops that assist her clients in building their confidence and forming a new creative outlook on life.

www.jeanninerivers.com

WHEN WOMEN GATHER, THE WORLD CHANGES

Laura Rubinstein, CHt

Today was a good day. I was energized. The weather was glorious. The flowers were bursting with color. I had a good night's sleep. I especially know when I'm feeling good because I have lots to share about things I'm excited about. However, not everything is rosy in my life (there's nothing tragic either). But yesterday my family had a minor incident with a neighbor that caused a great deal of concern. We didn't sleep well that night. Worry emerged about having to move, and that brought up all kinds of anxiety about the stability of everything from our jobs to retirement. I was very concerned that this situation could become a long-term issue. I knew I had to quell my anxiety. Luckily, my day happened to be filled with opportunities to connect with some of my dearest girlfriends. In fact, if these powerful female influences hadn't been there, my spirit would not have been lifted enough to rise above and dissipate the anxiety lingering in our home.

First was a morning call with my casual mastermind group. We each typically share the contributions we intend for ourselves, our family, community, and causes. The gift of sharing with those who believe in and support each other created a net of strength and belief in myself. I felt inspired by one member who revealed her global vision for creating sustainable communities. When I shared this with my husband, he seemed interested. It put his attention on something that he values and seemed to ease his stress.

Next I went for a walk with three women friends who are passionate about making a difference in various ways: one with entrepreneurs, one with dysfunctional families, and one with women. We discussed very personal family dynamics and helped ease anxiety for one friend. We had no agenda other than to share and support where requested. The subtle yet

most powerful element of this day is the **knowing that these women are here for me no matter what.** This energizes my confidence as they are a safe place for my heart to come back to. I like to say they **"have my heart"** like someone would "have your back."

By the time I got back home, my anxiety was gone and that made a big impact in the whole mood of the house. Being with my girlfriends naturally quelled my own fear which was being triggered by the negative headspace that started the previous day. I was fortified by my community who I know has my heart whenever I need them.

I went for a second walk later with a dear friend who shared about co-housing training—which was, as it turned out, a great resource for my mastermind friend in developing her sustainable community. I could have thought of this as a simple, sweet day with good friends. However, from another perspective I gained strength just by being with my women friends, and possibilities expanded for me, my friends, our families, and our communities. The synergies and impact made possible included keeping me and at least one of my friends from going to a dark, anxious, emotional place. And this made for two less anxious people in the world. It was just one day and a couple of conversations. Imagine if more people felt that kind of support surrounding them, like a comforting blanket that is always there. Might there be several hundreds . . . even thousands . . . less anxious people in the world? Might it be a different world?

When we gather as women, we often seek advice, connection, and healing. **When we cultivate this connection intentionally with other women who "have our heart," the world shifts**—first in one's inner circle of family and friends, and then the ripple effect takes place. Then it spreads to the immediate community and other communities, and so on.

We've seen it with the "Me Too" movement. In 2006 the phrase was coined by one woman. And in 2017 a hashtag was popularized by millions of women sharing it on social media. A global movement occurred with the collective of women intentionally supporting each other.

We've seen young women such as Emma Gonzalez after the Parkland high school shooting in 2018 ignite the March For Our Lives movement. From her initial request to speak at a rally that was granted by another woman on the school board, she has continued to garner the support of so many fellow citizens. She has gone on to write a book, have a featured *New York Times* op-ed article (with almost every comment cheering her on).

No doubt if women continue to support her, our world will be cleaner, healthier, and safer.

Whose heart do you have? I hope it's every woman who comes in your path. If you see them anxious, if you know they need something, could you ask to help, offer a smile, or simply intend for them a little more love? **When we have someone's heart the way you have their back, we bring healing.** What if we listened from our heart to theirs? What if everyone started doing this consciously? Let's start this movement. When women collectively intention something, the world changes. Can you envision a world of more love, positivity, and kindness? Gather with your like-minded women. Listen from your heart. Know that they have the wisdom to create a better world—and lend your energy where you can.

This chapter is an excerpt from my book about the journey to feminine power. If you love the principle **"When Women Gather, The World Changes"** you'll enjoy the *Feminine Power Cards* wisdom deck (FemininePowerCards. com) that inspired this chapter. Gather your girlfriends, play with these cards, and discuss the principles and practices. They will bring you new awareness and healing, emerge more of your authentic power, and create a better world for all. Let me know how it goes.

Laura Rubinstein, CHt, Social Buzz Club founder, is an award-winning digital media and marketing strategist, certified hypnotherapist, speaker, and author of the Feminine Power Cards and bestselling book Social Media Myths BUSTED. *Laura also serves on the Leadership Team for Women Speakers Association and hosts the* WSA-TV Premier Show. *Look for her upcoming book on feminine power.*

www.transformtoday.com

I'M HERE . . . NOW WHAT?

Dr. Janet J. Sawyer

Have you ever asked yourself, "What's next for me?"

After I retired from being a middle school administrator, being laid off from my leadership consultant position, divorcing after thirty years of marriage, and moving to a new state and city, I found myself asking the question, "I'm here . . . now what?"

As I thought about that question, I asked myself, "What have I always wanted to do but didn't have the time? In the past ten years, what have people told me I should think about doing?" I had always wanted to be a speaker. And people said I should think about becoming a life coach. But then I asked myself, "What is a life coach?"

When researching life coaching, I found this description from Wikipedia:

Coaching is a form of development in which an experienced person, called a coach, supports a learner or client in achieving a specific personal or professional goal by providing training and guidance.

Well, when I read that, given my background and experience and having been involved with personal and professional growth and development for over forty-five years, becoming a life coach made a lot of sense. *This could be the right next step for me,* I thought, so I started to explore this new direction.

I decided to become certified as a life coach. As part of my training, I listened to many coaching sessions, some of those being with Tony Robbins, Jack Canfield, Patrice Washington, and Kevin Trudeau. As I listened, I heard the same thing from each one of them, over and over in their own way: Most people don't know what they want. They go through the day without any thought of what they really want.

I remember thinking, *That can't be true.* I decided to find out for myself, so I went for a walk to the shopping center across the street from where I lived. I talked to four women and two men, ranging in age from twenty-three to seventy-five.

The first person was a man in his seventies. We had a short conversation, and then I asked, "If you could do anything you wanted, what would you want to do?" He said, "Well, I don't want any bills. I don't want to have to work." I responded by saying, "Oh, I can understand what you're saying, but I didn't ask you what you didn't want. I asked you, 'What DO you want?'" He stopped, paused for a moment, and said, "Oh, um, that's a great question."

Next I began talking to a young woman in her twenties who worked in a small women's boutique. I asked her the same question. "If you could do anything you wanted, what would you want to do?" To my surprise she said, "Well, I don't want to work here. I don't want to work forty hours a week." And I said, "Oh, I can understand what you're saying, but I didn't ask you what you didn't want. I asked you, 'What DO you want?'" She paused and said, "Hmm . . . I've never been asked that."

As I continued, the same thing happened over and over again. Out of the six people I spoke to, not one person could tell me what they wanted in their lives. They all told me what they didn't want.

I thought that day, *What if I could come up with a way to teach people how to unlock, in their mind and heart, what they really want?* So, I decided to design a *Mirroring Your Vision®* experience that I first used for myself with great success. I believed that if I followed this process and it worked for me, it would work for others too!

In the beginning of creating the *Mirroring Your Vision®* experience, I made a vision board by cutting and gluing pictures from magazines on a poster board. From there I attached these pictures to a mirror instead of the poster board so I could see myself in the vision. I then decided to write exactly what I wanted on my mirror, instead of using the pictures, so that when I read it, I would be able to see myself in my vision more clearly.

That's when *Mirroring Your Vision®* was born. It's an eight-step process that will help you mirror your vision by becoming Self-Aware, Intentional, and Mindful as you get clear about how you want to live and work. I began coaching my clients using this process and guiding them through:

- Creating a life of their dreams and imaging the results they want
- Thinking BIG and actually mirroring their vision

- Committing to the Power of 48 (making very small goals every forty-eight hours toward your vision) and manifesting with the Magic of 68 (applying the Law of Attraction to your life)

When attracting your personal and professional goals, there are five virtues that will support you to attract the dreams you discover during your *Mirroring Your Vision®* process and experience. They are:

- Courage—embrace life fully
- Commitment—no holding back
- Perseverance—the will to carry on
- Faith—confidence that your life has a purpose
- Trust—positive expectation

Mirroring Your Vision® has become an invaluable resource for helping others create the life of their dreams, and so much more! I am thrilled that I have been able to create a business that allows me to coach entrepreneurs, students, parent groups, sales teams, and business leaders to create the vision for their businesses and personal lives. My clients discover the results they are looking for . . . and they are living their lives the way they want!

Are you ready to explore what you want? Are you ready to see yourself in your vision? Well, let's get started!

Janet J. Sawyer, EdD, is an educator, leadership development coach, personality styles specialist, and a published author. She is the CEO and founder of JJ Sawyer Consulting, LLC, where she specializes in coaching her clients how to apply strategies that will help them move forward when setting personal and professional goals.

www.jjsawyerconsulting.com

It's Never Too Early to Pursue Your Business: Hacks for Studentpreneurs

Alexis Schomer

One of the most critical things I learned as a "studentpreneur" was how to be extremely resourceful. If you combine drive and motivation with resourcefulness and critical thinking, nothing can stop you. Utilizing available resources is the key to moving forward on the journey to accomplish your goals. No matter where you are on your journey, believe that reaching your goal is possible and you can succeed. Whether you're a student or a seasoned executive, you can work on your mindset in order to optimize opportunities to your benefit.

As a student entrepreneur, you have many resources available. Don't let the moment get the best of you—don't tell yourself there's no way you can start a business while being a full-time student, working part-time, and maintaining a social life. The reality is that it is possible, and it actually is ideal. Being a student gives you more leverage than being in the workforce because of the resources available to you. For example, there are many student-only business competitions that provide non-dilutive funding, in-kind services, and many other prizes or incentives. As a student, you have access to professors with industry expertise who are essentially free consultants. You also have access to all of the free resources your university provides, such as printing, database access, survey software, sponsored tickets to events, and so on.

I started my first company during college, and I wish I had done it sooner. Yes, you will have to sacrifice some of your social life. Yes, you will have very long days. Yes, you will work in between classes. Yes, you will be thinking about your company nonstop. Yes, it is possible. And yes, it is worth it. Whether you're just starting out or you're almost at the end of your journey, one piece of advice that everyone can consume is "fail often and fail fast." The best learning experiences come from failure, and as an entrepreneur, you cannot be scared of failing. Take advantage of the opportunity to start working on your passion before the rest of the crowd. The earlier you start, the earlier you can fail, and the earlier you will succeed.

Another reason it's beneficial to start your company in college is that you don't have 100 percent of the responsibilities of a working professional. You're cut a lot of slack, get discounts, and generally don't have to worry about putting food on the table and supporting a family. Being a young entrepreneur has its perks; being younger, you can take more risks. Imagine if you decided to quit your job at forty years old with a family to support; the pressure is a lot higher, and you may not have the financial freedom to quit your existing job to start a business. Take advantage of having less responsibility and go for it.

It does not take a big investment to start building a company. In fact, I did it with almost no capital. Think of repurposing your current spending habits. For example, instead of spending $100 on coffee per month (or $100 on going out), invest that money in building your dreams and goals. Imagine what $100 could do if you put it toward a strategic plan to develop your business. You could pay for a website ($12/month), business cards ($50), and other beneficial items.

Growing up with technology has given today's young adults advantages over all of the generations before us. Technology is a core component of business and daily life. Generally speaking, millennials and generations proceeding are much more technically savvy than the preceding ones. Because of the importance and societal dependence on technology, we truly have an inside advantage.

When you're a student, your brain is like a sponge. You absorb information rapidly and quickly. This mindset is very powerful and can be used for business purposes as well as school. Absorb as much information as you can while you still think like a student.

You don't need to feel like you're alone in this process either. While driven young entrepreneurs are a rare breed, know that many before you, including myself, have paved the way for you—and it's a liberating path. Don't be scared; be excited! Reach out to mentors and entrepreneurs for advice. Get organized and strategically plan your milestones, which you can set monthly, daily, and weekly. You can turn your passion into a business with the right mindset. You can turn anything into a business if you're willing and able to pivot when necessary and learn from customer feedback. This is what's called the entrepreneurial mindset, and it can be learned. Shifting your mentality from identifying problems to seeing solutions is a game changer. Problems are just opportunities to create successful businesses around specific and purposeful solutions. This shift in mindset is the key to entrepreneurship and innovation.

Use this three-step challenge to help shift your mindset:

1. Write down every problem you think of, come across, or are frustrated by for an entire week.
2. Shortlist the top ten problems and think of solutions for each one.
3. Choose the one you feel most passionate about, and here you have an idea for a business. (Disclaimer: don't put money into this solution before you validate that customers would pay for it and it solves a real problem; make sure you learn more about validating your product and finding the right product/market fit).

I'll leave you with one last piece of advice: be open to change and do not become obsessed with your idea. It's likely that your vision may not be a perfect fit for the market, and you'll need to make some alterations to match market demand. Leave all bias at the door if you are truly passionate about what you're working on.

If you have an idea, passion, or curiosity for entrepreneurship, I encourage you to take the risk and start your journey today.

Alexis Schomer is a serial entrepreneur with a passion for solving problems through innovation. Born and raised in Los Angeles, she co-founded her first tech start-up while still in college. She is a frequent speaker at educational and motivational events, publishes, and is a consultant in addition to running her current company.

www.alexisschomer.com

AUTHENTICITY: A JOURNEY TO SELF-ACCEPTANCE

Crystal-Marie Sealy

Anger. Despite its reputation, it is a powerful indicator that boundaries have been violated. It motivates us to reinstate them. In sharing my journey to authenticity, I could have focused on extreme politeness, fear, or perfectionism, but a recent conversation with friend and actor Ida Jagaric led me to anger. Here, I share anger's damaging power, how debilitating it is to silence it, and how I address its flare-ups during self-discovery. I hope you take only what resonates and release what does not.

As a child, I always knew when the adults were angry, and shrank accordingly. My mother did not spank me or my brother, but others around us did. It seemed as though I got spanked for even sneezing. Once it was because my brother had a headache, and everyone thought I had caused it! I was hurt and angry, but children did not express anger when I was growing up. At around eight years old, I had had enough. I would still be good, but I would simply stop walking on eggshells. I did not of course, and at fifteen, walking on eggshells led to what seemed like a nervous breakdown at school—crying and laughing simultaneously and uncontrollably.

By the time I was an adult, I shrank in response to everyone's anger. "Do you have to do that? It is so annoying!" my colleague Bert yelled one day in the office cafeteria. As I attempted to stop sniffling, I replied, "Sorry. I'm allergic to whatever's in the air. I can't stop sniffling." I went home so angry that I had explained and worse, apologized. Why did I continue to suppress my own needs to diffuse others' anger?

I respond in anger as a last resort, so I reasoned that so must everyone else. If they were angry with me, then they must have good reason. This colored my relationships with friends, men, and those in authority. Eventually, my anger evolved to reach levels of either zero or five hundred miles per hour.

Now, I remained silent so that I did not overreact. Why was I shrinking and contorting myself? Simply because I was not a part of my *own* life.

I had not given much thought to myself, beyond not causing trouble, but authenticity awakens when you return to your life. It asks what you think, how you feel, and holds space for you to stand in the power of your response. On October 28, 2019, I wrote "There are several industries making a mint off of the fact that many of us are wired to respond with submission when being scolded" in my blog post "Reframing Authenticity without Resentment or Rebellion." It is great to stop submitting to others' anger, but authenticity diminished resentment for me—or the rebellious urge in others.

As a mother, I get nauseous when children are told to be polite when people are being rude to them, to respect their elders when they are forced into unwanted hugs and kisses, or to *shhh* them when their opinions are different. I believe these experiences warp our inherent values and beliefs, creating a society of adults who do not trust themselves. It leaves us at the mercy of advisors—media, influencers, gurus, coaches, consultants—who may not honor individual sovereignty or our inherent ability to govern our own lives well, in our own time.

Advisors who give clients "a kick in the pants" diminish personal power, intentionally or not. This hit home for me as well because several of my clients have survived similar advisors. Amazing, highly capable and powerfully inspiring men and women second-guessed themselves as a result. This changed my consulting practice. My *mindful* strategy still focuses on sustainable pricing, lean process, feasible schedules and client-centric social media, but it now incorporates natural rhythms, current habits and desires, honoring clients' individual sovereignty. As a keynote speaker, authenticity is now my primary topic. This has also strengthened my commitment to gentle, responsive, attachment parenting (maximal empathy, responsiveness, and physically connection) as far as my daughter needs to foster her security, confidence, and independence in the long-term.

What does all of this have to do with authenticity and self-acceptance? *Everything.* Giving personal power away to advisors, shrinking in the face of anger, and disregarding our own anger are all rooted in a lack of authenticity and self-acceptance. I personally had to shift my mindset to make time and space for self-discovery. Things take the time they take. I could not rush this. Slowing down made room for me to show up again in my own life. Facing myself more fully dredged up more draining emotions. Slowing down to face them offered me a far less grueling pace than my continuous-improvement, performance-driven persona.

When anger showed up alongside the freedom of self-discovery, it became subconscious resentment for me. It showed up when I realized that what held me back was nurtured, not inherent, when my loved ones rolled their eyes at my newfound freedom. Having those angry conversations with myself and then releasing that resentment reenergized me. I also finally appreciated how freeing the statement "Live and let live" truly is. Everyone is free to feel as they do, myself included. I am only responsible for myself. Releasing resentment created so much clarity around deeper self-acceptance and unconditional self-love. That empowered me to be completely authentic—at least in my more mindful moments—without apology, defense, or explanation. I am far more likely now to walk away from that guy in the office cafeteria, in peace, without resentment. Today I set the necessary boundaries, but without resentment.

My upcoming book goes deeper, but the key is to get to a place where we can stay in our power in the face of disapproval, without internalizing that disapproval. I've focused on anger in this chapter, but whatever makes you second-guess yourself, I encourage you to face it, release it, and replace it with self-acceptance. This awakens authenticity, creating calm confidence and sustained rejuvenation. May this awaken courage and excitement to further pursue your own truth, wherever your journey takes you.

Crystal-Marie Sealy, MBA, dedicated mom, keynote speaker, author, and strategy consultant, speaks on authenticity and mindful entrepreneurship—pricing, process, and feasible schedules. Crystal-Marie's strategy framework is based on nineteen years of service, with BMO and the Ontario government as past clients. Today she serves premium service professionals.

www.crystalmariesealy.com

BULLETPROOF

Alicia Smith

Getting shot through the liver with an AK-47 didn't kill me. It only made me stronger, right? I would argue that Nietzsche's original statement is only partially correct. Let's say what doesn't kill you—and you work relentlessly to overcome—makes you stronger.

Life as a child was easy. My parents were honest, hardworking people. My siblings and I always had everything we needed. I lived a sheltered, comfortable life. I was raised in faith; the thread of Christianity was woven intricately into my life. My childhood gave me all the tools I would need to fulfill my dream of becoming a professional dancer. I set that goal at the ripe old age of nine. I spent every waking moment of the next nine years working on fulfilling that dream. (Do you think maybe I was a little strong-willed and determined?) After high school, as a dancer on scholarship at the University of Arizona, life was good . . . only for it to be shattered shortly after I had "arrived."

So how did I, a young, driven, small-town woman, end up in the middle of a gang fight? Why did this happen to me? How could I reach my goals now? How could this experience possibly enhance or deepen the meaning of my life? The truth is, we all go through hardships and face seemingly impossible challenges. At some point, we all ask, "Why?"

When that stray bullet found its way to me, life as I knew it came to an abrupt halt; it was gone forever. Before the shooting, I was a vibrant, independent, twenty-one-year-old woman. After the shooting, I was completely incapacitated, literally unable to lift a finger. Trauma like that doesn't just damage a person physically; it tortures you mentally, emotionally, and spiritually. It finds its way into every nook and cranny, leaving you numb, helpless, and dead inside.

My wounds were horrendous; countless complications arose. I had a hole the size of a man's fist in my skeletal body. After fifteen abdominal surgeries, I had deep, dark circles under my lifeless eyes. My hair was falling out. I could not walk on my own. My heart was broken. My spirit was close behind. I mourned the life I had lost.

Drowning in my own sorrow and self-pity, I was at my lowest point. Each day hatred for the man who had done this to me grew and penetrated deeper into my soul. The darkness had a death grip on me. I had no hope. The events of that night had led me to become resentful of any and everything that crossed my path.

After endless soul-searching, I came to realize that I had a choice in all of this. I could not control what had happened or even what was going to happen. I could only control how I responded. My choice was quite simple. This was either going to make me bitter or better. We all have that choice. No matter what is taken, no one can take that away!

After that life-altering revelation, an emotional healing process began. I wrestled with the loss of the life I used to live, moving through anger, depression, and finally acceptance. Piece by piece I was being restored. Unfortunately, none of it mattered if I couldn't let go of what had happened.

It took me years to realize that forgiving the person who shot me didn't diminish what happened. It wasn't an acknowledgment that what the perpetrator did was acceptable. His reprehensible and thoughtless actions showed a complete disregard for human life; he couldn't care less about me. Yet I was the only one continuously being damaged by my resentment and hate. My lack of forgiveness continued to devastate me but didn't touch him. Forgiveness would allow me to let go of the anger that was encapsulating me. Forgiving my assailant would allow me to be free.

I was able to find peace and forgiveness in the most unusual way, in the most extraordinary circumstances. It was a moment that swept me clean, a moment that would change the trajectory of my life.

Life is hard. We tend to avoid and try to escape our difficulties. Instead, we must attempt to face our trials with courage. Not an easy task, I might add. Nevertheless, it allows us to seek the opportunity to grow because adversity can always be a catalyst for growth. Who wants to be who they were ten years ago? Not me. Of course, growth takes perseverance and faith.

Forgiveness? Forgiving requires strength—I believe from a power bigger than yourself.

My decision to vanquish my suffering transformed me. I learned that my inner attitude didn't have to reflect my outward circumstances. My life is not what I had expected, but whose is? That initial gunshot wound left me with less than a 1 percent chance of survival, but I didn't just survive—I fought, overcame, and thrived. I will never set aside the moments in life that have changed who I am. Neither should any of you. We all experience times in life that seem to destroy our lives and make us question everything we have ever believed. But we can't just fall victim to the circumstances life has handed us. We must rise above them.

Now my life is what I have chosen to make it. I still have dance, although it's very different from the aspirations of my youth. I have an amazing family, a devoted husband, and four children, including a miracle baby. All this has been afforded to me through the very circumstances I thought destroyed my life.

Furthermore, I now have a voice—a voice to speak on behalf of those who do not get the opportunity to speak for themselves due to violence. Most importantly, it is a voice to share my journey down the path of destruction and despair to peace, joy, and hope.

I guess what doesn't kill you will make you stronger . . . if you allow it to. It's in those times of tragedy that you can use what is perhaps one of the most powerful tools you have as a human: the will to live. To live and to triumph!

Alicia Smith is an inspirational speaker, author, dance and music teacher, wife, and mother. She works to help others that have faced tragedy by speaking and sharing her personal story of survival and accomplishment after being shot with an AK-47. Alicia believes that adversity can always be a catalyst for growth. You can read the full story of Alicia's struggle in her autobiography Thread.

www.aliciasmithspeaks.com

FROM HAIR LOSS TO SELF-LOVE

Cornelia Steinberg

On New Year's Day 2016, I was walking on the beach, all by myself. I was minding my thoughts, enjoying the breeze from the ocean, and feeling the sand under my feet, when I suddenly heard a "voice." It said: "You have a message."

I turned around, but there was nobody in earshot, and even if so, why would a stranger say something like this to me?

As I am writing my story for you today, after three-and-a-half years on this journey, I am finally getting an idea of what this message is.

It is a message about self-love, self-acceptance, and letting go of an image that I built to be accepted by others and to please them. I hope my story will inspire you and give you hope on your journey, wherever you might be.

In March 2016 I got a phone call that changed my life forever. A recent colonoscopy revealed that I had a three-centimeter tumor in my transverse colon. It was malignant.

In May 2016 I had surgery to remove the tumor, during which another smaller mass was found near my aorta. The surgeons determined it was too risky to surgically remove it. It could be treated instead with chemo.

My worst fear bolted through me: chemo equals hair loss! But the doctors told me that this chemo would not result in hair loss.

But by 2018, the cancer had come back twice. It was determined that I needed a different chemo, and with this one I WOULD lose my hair! I was devastated! I was crushed! I could not believe this was happening.

After I gave myself space to cry and be angry, I reflected on why this was such a trauma for me. Suddenly an image of an event from my childhood appeared in my mind. When I was growing up in the sixties in Germany, I sported a pixie cut which made me look like a boy. One day, when I was maybe eight or nine years old, I went to the pool, and the woman at the lockers gave me the BOYS' LOCKER key! Imagine that! I was hurt.

I think somehow, deep down inside, I made a decision in that moment to never, ever look like a boy again.

Over the next few years, growing into a teenager and young woman, I became a very feminine, cute, and sexy woman.

The day when I learned that hair loss was inevitable, sitting in my living room with the thought of soon losing my hair, all those old childhood fears came right back, washing all over me. What would I look like? What would people think? Bald, with a high forehead and a big nose?

I was devastated.

A few weeks later, when all my hair was gone, looking in the mirror one day, I saw this bald, skinny me with cancer. I felt so raw, so naked and vulnerable. I felt stripped of everything—my femininity, my personality, and the image I had built for myself. It was all gone!

Sure, you might say that beauty is really on the inside, but when you are bald and skinny with cancer, this truly sounds like some idiot's bumper sticker.

But something happened over the next few weeks.

Every time I looked at my reflection, all I saw was that head with no hair, not feminine, not pretty. **I knew I had a choice.** I could stay in my "ugly duckling story" or I could focus my attention on what was pretty about me! And as a coach, I chose the latter. People have told me over the years that I had really beautiful eyes. I was able to see that now. I had to admit, my eyes were beautiful. I decided to emphasize my eyes by putting on eye shadow. And I chose to wear bigger earrings to frame my face.

I was beginning to like my new looks.

With that, I noticed a *change happening inside me.* A new confidence was growing inside me. A confidence that had been there all along, while I was busy holding that cute, feminine image to please others. I noticed myself in random situations reacting in a different way, a stronger, more "I know my place" kind of way.

I felt a new sense of myself. I felt a deep sense of appreciation and love for myself awakening deep inside my heart. It was exciting. It was comforting.

And then my hair started to grow back, little by little. I was ecstatic. And it was dark, not gray! When my head was covered with hair that was about a quarter of an inch long, I decided to ditch the beanie. Oh my, that first time going without a head piece, feeling the wind touching my soft hair, the warmth of the sun on my skin! I felt so free; it was a divine moment. I was in awe of my body.

And then my daughter caught me by surprise. She told me how proud she was when I went to church without my beanie the first time shortly thereafter. Yes, it did take courage to "come out" this way, not looking like my old self, the blonde, cute, and feminine me.

But you know what? This new hairstyle was perfect for the new me, the woman I was becoming—stronger and more confident, knowing her role in the world. It seemed as though the cancer had been the trigger to introduce a "new me," or rather, the me I was meant to be. Losing my hair and facing the adversity of cancer had brought up fears, limiting beliefs, and images that no longer served me.

And then it became crystal clear that all these years I had been busy building an image so I would be accepted by others. But this ordeal with losing my hair took down some old belief systems and brought forth the confidence that had been there all along. I realized that it doesn't matter what other people think of me; it matters what I think about MYSELF—and it is up to me to accept and love myself just the way I am!

Cornelia Steinberg was born and raised in Germany and has been learning and teaching self-development for thirty-plus years. When she was diagnosed with colon cancer in 2016, her life came to a screeching halt and would never be the same. Through this journey she has learned to accept and love herself for who she is. As a speaker and author, Cornelia wants to share her story and instill a spark of hope with her audience.

www.corneliasteinberg.com

Editors' Note: As this book was going to print, we were saddened to learn of Cornelia's passing. A valued member of Women Speakers Association, she will be greatly missed and leaves behind a powerful legacy of strength and hope.

It Really Does Take a Village

Karen Strauss

Barely glancing at me, the technician told me to go back to the waiting room as they needed to get more pictures of me. When you have had as many mammograms as I have, I knew what that meant.

I sat and waited, sat and waited some more. . . . I was petrified, anguished, paralyzed. I kept going up to the front desk and asking when they would call me back. I waited another thirty minutes, and finally I could not breathe--my adrenaline was pumping and I thought I was going to faint.

So I ran! Out of the double doors—out into the street where the sun was shining that warm July day. I ran to the bus to take me home so I could put my head under the covers, irrationally thinking that if the words weren't spoken, I wouldn't have the dreaded "c" word.

On the bus my cell phone kept ringing. When I got home, the phone was still ringing. I had several messages from the lab telling me it was urgent I go back. I finally called them and scheduled my appointment for the next morning at 8:00 a.m. Next I called my best friend. She dropped everything and listened and then insisted that she go with me the next day. It didn't hurt that she is a women's health provider and knows her way around an x-ray.

They confirmed that I had breast cancer. The bad news was that it had already started to spread outside the duct, but the cancer was really small, and it had been caught early.

I will never forget the walk home, with my friend Susan holding my hand. She said, "You are going to be fine. It will be a rough journey for a while, but you will be just fine. You will come to see this as just a bump in the road."

Well, I am not going to lie. It felt like much more than a bump in the road during that long, dreadful year. The biopsy, endless meetings with surgeons, oncologists, my primary doctor . . . Susan was with me through all of it. I was so grateful to her; she was my advocate. She took notes; she could hear what the doctors were saying, while I could barely listen.

Finally we found the right team. I had the surgery—I needed a mastectomy. I woke up in the hospital to four worried faces trying to put on a brave front: my brother and sister-in-law, Susan, my cousin. . . . Everybody said at once, "It went great!" That was the beginning of my transformation, although I didn't know it yet.

You see, I had always been a very independent woman. Even when I was very young, I could always "do it myself." I didn't need anyone to help me; I was the one who people turned to when they needed to talk about their problems. I always saw needing help from someone as weak. I was the strong one. I was not going to be vulnerable—I would manage just fine!

I could take care of managing my business, my clients, my employees, my co-op, my house in the country, my dog—and now my cancer. This was just one more thing . . . right?

Well, I could not have been more wrong! I didn't realize what a big deal this was, and I needed to focus every bit of attention on getting well. From surgery to setting up the chemo treatment, and then living with the effects of the chemo itself—the nausea, the fatigue, the memory loss—I don't know how I would have made it through without my family, good friends—surprisingly even those that weren't such good friends.

For instance, one person (now an Oscar winner for the movie *Birdland*) who I knew from the dog park called me and offered to take my dog, Izzy, to the park anytime I wanted. I did not know him very well at that point, and his generous offer floored me.

Similar offers came. A woman in my building is a makeup artist, and when I had a swanky holiday party to attend, she offered to do my makeup—complete with false eyelashes!

And one night, when I decided it was time to cut the remaining hair on my head (a very emotional decision for me), my friend (whose husband works on Broadway) brought over one of her friends who cuts hair professionally for Broadway productions. They made it fun—we had champagne and hors d'oeuvres.

One neighbor, who I knew just to say hello to, came to my apartment every night while I was going through chemo to check on me, see if I needed anything, and offer to walk Izzy. This was a lifesaver, since by then I was pretty wiped out and sometimes couldn't even make it off the couch, let alone get dressed in five layers, dress Izzy, and walk out in 10-degree weather so Izzy could do his business.

I could go on and on about the generosity and support offered to me by friends, family, and acquaintances who were ready and willing to do something, anything, to help me. And for the first time in my life, I let them! Wow! What a feeling—I went from feeling guilty to feeling grateful and appreciative of the fact that so many people wanted to support and help me. All I had to do was say yes and give them a task.

So many people came to sit with me during the four hours each week I had my chemo treatment. My friends who thought they were stand-up comedians practiced on me, their captive audience. Some of my friends came to gossip, or spill their problems, or just discuss world events. I was SO grateful not to have to talk about "how I was feeling," or about my illness in general. It made the time fly by.

I have never forgotten this lesson. I no longer want to be a loner, to have to make decisions by myself, to not allow myself to be vulnerable. This has stood me in good stead to grow my business as well as become more intimate in my personal relationships.

I've learned that life is more fun when I let people in. I no longer feel the weight of the world on my shoulders. I know I have mentors, friends, advisors, and loved ones who will keep me grounded, supported, and constantly aware that I do not have to go through life alone.

It really does take a village —and I am deeply and profoundly grateful!

Karen Strauss has worked in publishing for more than thirty years and has held management and marketing positions at major publishing houses, including The Free Press, Crown, Random House, and Avon. Karen founded Hybrid Global Publishing in 2011 to help authors, speakers, and entrepreneurs get their message out by writing and publishing a book. She offers publishing, distribution, and marketing services for organizations and individual authors.

www.hybridglobalpublishing.com

Dare to Be Uniquely Yourself

Cate Tuitt

As women we often are taught to fit into gender roles. So how do we learn more about who we are? We have to get to know ourselves, what matters to us, and what makes us want to jump out of bed in the morning to begin another day.

Life is not just about struggle—we are meant to thrive. Yet we are often racked with fears. How do we turn our pain into power?

In 2009 I had a near-death experience. As I took time to recover, art and painting helped me to reflect on how precious life is, and that has led me to share with you my five top tips to dare to be uniquely yourself.

1. Stay true to yourself. Identify your values and what you care about. What are you passionate about? What means a lot to you in life? After you've identified your values, if you don't feel comfortable engaging in certain things you used to do, don't beat yourself up over it.

You can change your mind over life. You may decide to be a vegetarian, so invites to dinner mean letting meat lovers know. Or you may want to source your clothes more ethically.

Surround yourself with people who will support you and care for you in this journey.

2. To know who you are, first you have to forget who they told you that you were. Were you ever called naughty when you were a child? Did someone tell you you were bossy? Maybe someone called you a pushy mother. Own it—others' words can give you courage and drive you to be uniquely you.

I remember as a child growing up being told at school, "Your mother is a widow, and you may as well give up now with education," and "Why are you bothering with your exams?"

To know who we are, first we have to forget who they told us we were.

Silence the critical voices in your head that say you are not worthy, that you are an imposter. Forget whatever has led to you feeling down or undeserving. You can dare to defy your detractors and realize that you are not an imposter in a room full of people who tell you they are more clever than you, or more worthy than you of success, even if they attended the best colleges and universities or were born into wealth.

We all have our own talents and qualities, and you can dare to be uniquely yourself.

3. Think about what you want for your future. Many of us are taught that it is a selfish act to think about ourselves, to put ourselves first. Especially as women, however, for our own health and needs, it is not selfish to put ourselves first sometimes. The world for women is still heavily weighted against us.

Yet we are still innovative, making healthy meals on a tight budget and feeding our families. We can take these skills from the kitchen table into the boardroom and thus drive the future.

Remember that change will not happen overnight. Commit to changing your outcomes and those of others for the better.

Distance yourself from negative thinking, and don't punish yourself for the mistakes you made in the past. As we are human, we all make mistakes.

4. Don't merely follow the rules—but keep it legal! Of course, with a degree in law, you would expect me to tell you to keep it legal. But unwaveringly following the rules won't give you the results you desire to see the change you want in your life.

We cannot continue to follow outdated rules that have not been made by us or for us. Learn about tax laws and pensions. Spend time thinking about your later years and start saving now and planning within your means.

You are not an imposter. You deserve all your achievements and successes.

Always remember that self-care is vitally important. Keep living your true, unique self. You don't have to buy expensive beauty treatments. You can blend avocados and use your own ingredients for face masks like I do. Tell yourself every day that you deserve happiness and you are worthy.

5. Strive for economic and financial empowerment. None of us can see into the future, and we don't know what will befall us. But we can try to get ourselves into shape financially, even if the economy does not benefit us. Many women I speak to feel like victims of economic forces.

I founded a financial co-operative in London in 2000, as part of an anti-poverty initiative. It is owned by its members; all the profits are invested back into the credit union. It offers micro finance loans to women from a variety of social and economic backgrounds. I was inspired by my mother to establish it, as most of the world's co-op credit unions are in the Caribbean.

Maybe you could also do the same in your communities to give both women and men financial freedom and encourage them to save and budget.

If you have been out of work, use that time as an opportunity to be uniquely yourself and take that art class or do that boxing fitness you always wanted to do but never had the time!

Your favorite recipes could be just the nutritional value that someone needs to get their health back on the road to recovery. Have you considered that this could be your new small business?

There are many opportunities for you to gain new experiences. If your children have left home and you have some spare time on your hands, why not consider new ways to dare to be uniquely yourself?

This will have ripple effects—like a stone dropped in water, the ripples will go deep, far, and wide. You can show others that they too can shine outside the gender constructs of their circumstances and be uniquely who they were meant to be!

Cate Tuitt is a motivational speaker, trainer, and consultant. She studied law at university in London and worked for over twenty-five years in justice and law. She was also the CEO of a women's shelter in London. Her experience with clients gave Cate insight into the power of art, painting, and nutrition to use as a resource to overcome trauma.

www.catetuittbooks.com

Growing Grit: The ABCs of Dealing with Adversity

Lois Wagner

And I wished I could be spontaneous and happy like my little sister.
She always smiled with her whole face and my smile never reached my eyes.
Lizz Huesmann, *Dancing in the Shadows*

Why do certain things happen to us and not to others? Why do we face the same negative experiences over and over and over again? These are questions to be answered another day. Today is about how to survive and thrive after life's disruptions—how to build grit and resilience and to develop your mojo.

I have lived an exciting, adventurous, productive, and yet challenging life. From a dysfunctional early life filled with alcohol and abuse to an adult life of divorce and rape. From a debilitating childhood illness to physical disabilities in adulthood. From being overlooked for opportunities in my career to being fired, retrenched, and forced into retirement. I've been financially poor and in debt. I've gone bankrupt as an entrepreneur and started and closed another business. And in between, I have experienced being the victim of multiple robberies, the death of loved ones, and accidents both big and small.

And here I am, smiling. Smiling with my whole face. With my whole being. Follow me on my journey and find your smile.

Accept *Adversity*. I was attacked, raped, and left for dead. I did not sit back and wallow in self-pity; instead I accepted the pain, the anger, the bitterness, and yes, even the hatred. I felt the emotions in all their intensity but did not stay there. When forced into early retirement with no pension or savings plan, I was enraged. I lashed out. But I did not stay there.

It helps to feel the negative emotion or thought pattern. Rate the emotion on a scale of one to ten. And then pause in the feeling. Consider and understand the rejection.

Change Your *Belief.* Overweight and unfit, trekking more than half a mile almost completely vertically to see the Tiger's Nest Monastery in Bhutan, the locals took bets that I would not make it. That was their feeling, not mine. The fact is, it made me more determined to reach the top, which I did.

It was not my fault I lost my job. So many victims of rape believe they were to blame. That is not a fact; it is a feeling. Recognize the truth behind the emotion. What is the evidence? Is this a fact or is it a feeling? Embrace the negative and turn it into a positive.

Examine the *Consequences.* How was my regret for closing a successful business going to help me? Who was I hurting by hating and wanting to seek revenge for the rape, the lost job, the divorce? Only myself.

It is best to examine the consequences or implications of the situation and understand the negative impact of these emotions and thoughts.

Dispute **and** *Debate.* I kept having accidents. These included falling off a dog sled, rolling a snowmobile, falling off my bicycle, drifting out to sea while scuba diving, and many more. Instead of feeling sorry for myself, I turned these stories into stories of resilience, of survival, of picking myself up and starting over. After I was raped, I worked at changing the world. I started petitions, led marches, and helped lobby to get the laws changed. I developed a focus to make the world a safer place for women.

Challenge your view, argue with yourself, and change your narrative by focusing on the lessons you've learned and the positive preferred emotion or outcome you desire.

Energize **Yourself.** "By speaking at high paying events around the world, I do what I love and help and inspire others to achieve success and happiness" is one of my favorite affirmations.

Create and repeat your own affirmations. Emotionally set the intention for the day. Energize yourself and choose a positive course of action. Get moving physically.

Follow **Your Dreams,** *Forgive,* **and** *Fly Free.* Once you have faced your emotions, considered the consequences, and set your intentions, it is time to take action. It's important to start working toward achieving that affirmation, that aspiration, that goal.

These days I am giving presentations, both free and paid for. I am sharing my stories. I am coaching, inspiring, and supporting others. I am following my dreams.

I was the first person in South Africa to take advantage of a new law allowing victims (I prefer to call myself a thriver) of crime to attend a parole hearing. I forgave the rapist who had spent fourteen years in a maximum-security prison. This was the most freeing emotion that I have ever experienced. I forgave a business partner that betrayed me. And others. And myself.

By forgiving, you break the bonds that tie you to the other person, and you fly free!

Grit and *Gratitude.* Grit is my drive, my passion, my perseverance. Grit is my persistence that keeps me interested and focused on my goals and aspirations. As a child, I wanted to write and act. It took me a long time, but I always had this vision. I never gave up. And now, finally, in my sixties I am realizing this dream. I am so grateful for the challenges and hardships I have faced. They have given me the material to use in fulfilling my vision of writing and speaking on stage.

Practicing gratitude daily increases your self-esteem and energy, makes you more optimistic, and enhances your empathy and relationships. Live with gratitude.

H to Z. The balance of the ABCs includes H—focusing on *happiness,* R—my *resilience,* my optimism, that gives me renewed determination and greater strength to face life's challenges, and Z—stepping outside of my comfort *zone* to make a difference in the world.

You, too, can survive and thrive and find your smile!

Lois Wagner is a curious traveler, thriver, inspirational speaker, executive business coach, leadership consultant, and mentor. As a certified Conversational Intelligence® (C-IQ) coach, she facilitates individual and group coaching interactions and immersion workshops. Her stories motivate the audience to develop a growth mindset, to build their resilience and grit, to energize their mojo, and to achieve their personal best.

www.loiswagnercoaching.com

IMAGE 360

Karyn Wiles

Hey there! I see you. Well, maybe not literally, but figuratively! I see you because in many ways I am a lot like you. I used to run from my many gifts and talents until one day I couldn't run anymore. For years, I would have what I thought were good ideas, but I was waiting for validation from something or someone. Then the light bulb went off, and I just HAD to move! And move I did!

Are you in a similar place where you know things are not quite right? Have you been wanting that new job, looking to write that book, or maybe trying to get the courage to boss up and make your dream of starting a business come true?

So what is holding you back? Are you too scared to move? That's OK. As I said before, we have some things in common. I'm very familiar with that big, hairy, scary thing that often keeps us stuck in a rut and frozen in place. Yes, that thing called FEAR! I have found that while I sometimes haven't been able to make big leaps, I've been able to take infinitesimal steps. Those are fancy words for baby steps, y'all! The funny thing about baby steps is that you'll have many small accomplishments. Those accomplishments will add up and each step helps to build your momentum and confidence.

As a corporate image consultant, I find that some people are challenged by what to wear, but they're often in need of some other skills that round out what I like to call the four points of image. This inspired me to create the I-Box. The focus is on style/image, etiquette, soft skills, and personal branding. Let's take a look at the importance of each of the four sections:

1. **Image.** Your life is crazy busy, and you're always on the go. You just don't have time to care about your appearance, right? WRONG! How you show up in the world speaks to how you feel about yourself and provides an outward indicator of your self-esteem or lack thereof. Sadly, it is sometimes considered to be an indicator of the quality of your work.

Finding items to suit you may have been challenging in the past. I get it! The following questions have been designed to get you thinking about some changes that may be needed in order to advance both you and your career. The goal is for you to shine, so you can SOAR!

1. Do you find it challenging to get ready in the morning?
2. Do you feel your career or business has been hindered because of your appearance?
3. Do you feel comfortable and confident in your appearance?
4. Do you feel you could benefit from a style update/refresh?
5. Do you often feel like you have nothing to wear?

2. Etiquette. Etiquette is a big topic in the workplace right now and has been for some time. There is even a National Business Etiquette Week. Business norms vary across industries and locales, but there are definitely some universal things to keep in mind. While some of these points may just be a reminder from the old school days of charm schools, Girl Scouts and debutante balls, it can't hurt to have a refresher course.

1. Dress appropriately. (See, style really IS important!)
2. Always say "please" and "thank you."
3. Be present and avoid phone usage during meetings.
4. Offer a handshake and make eye contact.
5. Give cues that show you're paying attention.
6. Send customized, handwritten thank-you notes.
7. Proofread emails for grammar and typos.
8. Be polite and professional.
9. Always be on time.
10. Show respect for shared areas and items.

3. Soft Skills. Soft skills can be defined as those skills that are a part of you. More specifically, they refer to your people skills. In contrast, hard skills are taught and are most often learned in school or from previous work experience. My research noted several different sets of soft skills. The following are just some of the top skills that are currently sought after in today's ever-changing marketplace.

- Collaboration
- Strong work ethic
- Enthusiasm
- Attention to detail

- Effective communication
- Works well under pressure
- Integrity
- Time management
- Creativity
- Self-confidence

4. Personal Branding. A personal brand is the experience that people have with you and what you represent. It's how you package your various skills, talents, personality, and values with the goal of building your reputation and network in the marketplace. Ultimately it comes down to what you want to be known for and how you want to convey your value to others.

What is your unique value proposition? Better yet, how have you put your signature (wink) on a product or service to make it more appealing than something currently being offered? The packaging that you share with the world is like your online business card.

Why should someone choose you? More importantly, are people even able to FIND you? The message you craft should be consistent, honest, and reliable across all platforms. As you fine-tune your message and it begins producing the desired results, you will gain more confidence, which others will see and most likely respond to in a positive and financially rewarding way. At the center of it all is YOU!

There is an age-old saying that you only have one chance to make a good first impression. I agree, and I would like to add that you only have the gift of one life. Don't you owe it to yourself to be, do, and have everything that you've ever wanted?

Be You . . . Be Bold . . . Be Confidently FABULOUS!

Karyn Wiles is the chief style officer of the Signature Image Group, a Division of Styled by Wiles. As a corporate image consultant and personal brand strategist, Karyn helps clients develop a signature style that is uniquely their own.

www.karynwiles.com

SOARING WITH HAPPINESS AND JOY

Jennifer S. Wilkov

I have been rising and falling and rising again all my life. I am a miracle and have experienced and made miracles since I was born. I have been dubbed "The Make It Happen Girl" by many ever since I was a little girl. Yes, I'm the one they say can turn lemons into lemonade—every time. I've been accused of having GRIT, an acronym for Guts, Resilience, Integrity, and Tenacity. I have learned that "Man plans . . . and God laughs."

I'm the girl who was diagnosed with Crohn's disease at age ten—the only person in my family to ever have this diagnosis. I suffered with this chronic and dehumanizing illness for over twenty years. I'm the same girl who decided that after living with Crohn's for more than 20 years, I would stop experiencing it. I'm the girl who beat the odds, befuddled the medical professionals, got off every drug I was on in six months after my second bowel resection, and cured myself. I've never had another experience with Crohn's disease since 2001.

When you decide to have new experiences, be brave. Be bold. Be BRILLIANT! Like me. In March 2016, I successfully produced my first conference called Speak Up Women at the United Nations. On May 25th, I completed the Grand Canyon Rim to Rim Hike (23.5 miles from the North Rim to the South Rim that I did in 15.5 hours in a single day). Yes, I'm an elite hiker. On July 10th, I summited Mt. Kilimanjaro on my second climb of that mountain, ten years after the first time I climbed it when I missed the summit by about 800 feet. This time I succeeded.

I was on top of the world . . . literally! I came down from the summit—and I had learned A LOT. What I didn't realize was that I had been fortified for what would be some of my biggest challenges yet. I just didn't see any of them coming.

Being a person who has been imbued and infused with RESILIENCE, I was able to withstand, endure, and make it through what followed my descent of the mountain: a diagnosis of Advanced Stage IV Non-Small Cell Lung Cancer just four short months later. After the diagnosis, my first thoracic oncologist at Memorial Sloan-Kettering Cancer Center, the chair of the department, ordered a port to be implanted in my body, followed by eight infusions of chemotherapy. I was highly allergic to these drugs, but he didn't stop. I nearly died from the side effects of the treatment right before his eyes in July 2017. I was flirting with six feet under after being on top of the world nearly one year earlier.

Amidst the crescendo of this overwhelming experience and first of seven near-death experiences that would occur between January 2017 and November 2019, I never lost a client through any of this—not one. As Yogi Berra said, "It ain't over till it's over." When you experience devastating situations, do what I did: brush yourself off. Smile. Connect with your inner strength and get back in the game. Don't stop playing till they tell you to go home and your time is really up.

Two years later, after recovering from my first two near-death experiences, the death of my cat, the adoption of a new rescue kitty, a fire in our apartment, and getting married, I found myself again facing the reality of cancer and the ugly challenges it presented for me to navigate. By mid-March 2019, I wasn't functioning well cognitively. On April 4th, 2019, I was rushed to the hospital, delirious with a fever of almost 103 degrees and no understanding of who I was, where I was, or what day it was. I couldn't say who the president was, or name the days of the week, or count to ten. For the next week, my husband planned my funeral, picked out my coffin, and started planning hospice for me in the event I survived. One week later, I rolled over in my hospital bed, weakly raised my hand and softly said, "Hi!" when my husband walked into the hospital room.

From April to July, I went on to experience the next four near-death experiences (all very different from one another). On July 19, I celebrated a one-year vow renewal ceremony with my husband, commemorating our first Jewish year anniversary. Then from July to October, I experienced the deaths of ten people in my world. TEN.

One of these deaths was the death of my ninety-year-old father-in-law, who was a great man. Following his death, my husband and his family immediately became emotionally abusive toward me. They became toxic in every way imaginable. During this same period, I actually had a miraculous surgery to remove the port that had been used for the chemotherapy infusions that nearly killed me. In my mind's eye this was an exorcism of sorts—cutting out all the toxicity, anger, upset, hurt, and fury I felt about the oncologist's negligence and total disregard for me as well as the same feelings I had about my husband and his family. I was done with all of it and all of them.

In October, the surgery was nothing short of miraculous. I had it done in Memorial Sloan-Kettering's main operating room with no general anesthesia and no colonoscopy anesthesia. I was brought just to the edge of twilight and heard the whole thing from start to finish. I left about twenty minutes afterward with no painkillers, and I didn't experience any bruising, inflammation, or infection. I was one of the few who gets to have her port *taken out* because I didn't need it anymore. I *really am* miraculously healing from cancer, right before everyone's eyes.

After my father-in-law died, I told my husband I was going to leave him *four times* during the three months that followed. I had just regained my balance, strength, endurance, and stamina when this incredible storm of emotional abuse toward me blew in. The overwhelming insanity was so detrimental to my health and well-being . . . and to my business. Thoughts about my husband and his family's meddlesome and troubling narcissistic behaviors kept me up at night. When I would get up to work in the wee hours of the night when I couldn't sleep, my husband would follow me, talking with me and distracting me from my efforts to just get something done even at that hour of the day. It was incessant interruption after incessant interruption.

At the end of one of my healing treatment sessions in November, I shook my head from the fog I had been in and shouted, "I'M MOVING!" I called my mother and said, "I'm moving!" I went home and said to my husband, "I'm moving—with or without you. I'm moving!" Five weeks later, we moved on up to a deluxe apartment in the sky—on the twenty-first floor. I left everything behind me—the diagnosis, the fire, the cancer, the near-death experiences, all ten deaths, and the nasty, narcissistic, and mean-spirited behaviors of my husband and his family. I left brownstone Brooklyn living and all its "charms" behind so I could soar with happiness and joy on the twenty-first floor in a deluxe 24/7, full-service building twenty blocks away for the difference of just a couple hundred dollars a month.

Trust the Universe. It's what people with RESILIENCE do. It's the Feng Shui philosophy: Change your space; change your life. That's what I did, and you can do it too.

Each of us chooses the experiences we will have in this life. What "happens" to us is only 10 percent of the experience. Once an event occurs, no matter how big or small, it is how you choose to perceive it and the meaning you give it and then how you choose to handle it that is 90 percent of the equation as to how you will actually experience it.

RESILIENCE is about handling it—handling the meaning you give what has occurred. It is a recipe for successfully moving through each situation with grace, integrity, and as much peace of mind as possible.

RESILIENCE involves being committed to resolving a situation with as much resourcefulness as you can muster. It happened. It's over. You cannot change what happened, and you cannot take back what you did or said. Neither can anyone else. You can only change how you individually are going to choose to experience it now and move through the rest of it so you can soar again with happiness and joy.

RESILIENCE requires expression. In order to soar again with happiness and joy, you MUST speak up for yourself, your position, and your truth in the situation. You must express your feelings, thoughts, hopes, and fears. You must be honest with yourself and with others. You must be willing to listen to others and allow them to express themselves without judgment, and you must not take anything they say personally. It is not about you; it's about them. You must take 100 percent responsibility for your words, actions, and deeds during the event. If someone indicates that you have hurt them in any way, emotionally or physically, apologize freely and acknowledge that they have indicated that something you did caused them pain. Apologize for it whether you did it knowingly or unknowingly, consciously or unconsciously, intentionally or unintentionally, so you can easily glide through the incident without harboring any resentment or causing someone else to do this. **The apology is the turnstile that allows the relationship to effortlessly continue without any detours from drama caused by distractions from either person's ego's need to be right.** It is simply about allowing each other to make mistakes and missteps in the relationship, inform each other and apologize when they happen, and move swiftly through them without the need to make a pitstop to "work it out."

The truth is: Only I can tell YOU what I am experiencing during any event and how it feels FOR ME. Only I can tell YOU if something you do hurts me in some way. Only I can tell YOU if I don't like something you made for dinner or if you picked out a piece of clothing that I would never wear. Only I can tell YOU how to love me because only I know how I experience love and what makes me feel loved. You must speak up and express yourself clearly in order to a) get what you want and need and b) clearly ask for help and be resourceful with the people around you who want to love and support you in the ways you desire.

Being resilient demands that you have integrity—that when you express yourself, your words and your actions match. In order to rise after free falling, your ticket back to the top is paid for with your honest actions, words, and deeds. Integrity is essential, no matter what the circumstances and situation are.

RESILIENCE is not possible when you harbor resentment. You must be willing to let go of whatever you are harboring and holding on to so tightly that you are terrified to let go of it. "It" could be your marriage, your job, your apartment or house, your friends, your pet, your profession, your industry, your clothes, your jewelry, your hair, your hearing, your sight, and even your mobility. The more quickly you surrender to what has occurred, the faster you will be able to focus on how you will resolve the situation and circumstances using the resources you have and by asking for the resources you need—even the ones you don't know to ask for.

Balance is the essence of RESILIENCE. You must be able to both be in the weeds and get out of the frame and distance yourself from the event so you can see all sides of the situation. You must become emotionally intelligent about what has occurred and not make decisions until you feel balanced. We are all human. We say things that are hurtful to others. We respond to things that are said to us that feel hurtful when we feel like we are under siege. Step aside, get out of the way of karma, and regain your balance—in your mind, body, spirit, and soul. Don't ever let anyone steal these from you. You are responsible to yourself for keeping these safe, fit, and well taken care of in this lifetime.

One of the key ingredients in RESILIENCE is contribution. Contribution is all about asking the question "How can I best support YOU?" and letting someone else tell you what feels good for them and what they need. It is the difference between walking around in your world and wondering, "What's in it for ME?" "What have you done for ME lately?" and "What can you do FOR ME?" and asking someone what you can contribute to their life today. Asking "How can I best support YOU?" opens up the communication superhighway between you and someone else—whether it's a spouse, a family member, a parent or child, a friend, an in-law, a business colleague, a professional colleague, or a stranger.

The act of contributing to others opens your heart, mind, and spirit to the happiness and joy of creativity. It is the window into answering the question: How can I make someone else smile? How can I help someone else see that the world is a wonderful, glorious place? It's not about what's happening to ME right now. In every situation I have ever been in, **one of my most tried and true ways of lifting myself out of it was by lifting others. I truly believe that we are all here to help one another live the lives we imagine.**

Each of us has a journey we are destined to make in this life, regardless of how long or short it is, and no matter what highs and lows it entails. Contribution to our own lives, spirits, and souls comes from creatively being able to navigate the bumpy and bright path that has been mapped out for each of us. You have your own path you are traversing and experiencing. I have mine. I'll never see, hear, smell, touch, or taste these experiences the same way. It's humanly impossible for me to do this. Let someone else tell you what they want from you so you can give it to them endlessly . . . and they in turn will love you forever for giving it to them in the ways they asked you to. Now why would anyone not want to do that? It's so much easier than having to read someone's mind.

As you employ these other attributes of RESILIENCE, you will evolve. You will inspire others to be resilient, as they will see you as someone who is extraordinary and who is living a life they admire and aspire to want to live. You will illustrate for them the lives they can now imagine.

The difference between those who are resilient and those who admire those who are resilient is this: the ones who are resilient BELIEVE first. We don't need to see it to believe. We BELIEVE "it" is already possible and done before we even begin. The admirers and aspirers? They need to SEE it first in order to believe it. That's the difference! That's why some people soar and others . . . well, sometimes never get to. Once you cross over to the beautiful, positive, rose-colored side of the street and take in the view, you will evolve and find it's quite peaceful here. Not much drama; it's simply not appropriate. We're all too busy making our way respectively and helping one another other out as much as we can so we can all live the lives we each imagine.

The heart of RESILIENCE is endurance. It's a necessity. Your level of endurance must be high—teetering off the charts. What's endurance, you ask? I like the definition I found in Wikipedia: "Endurance is the ability of an organism to exert itself and remain active for a long period of time, as well as its ability to resist, withstand, recover from, and have immunity to trauma, wounds, or fatigue." You must be able to continue forward in the face of distress, discomfort, decimation, and despair. You must go on.

When you are resilient and embody its characteristics, you cannot help but soar with happiness and joy! Our lives change every day. Every day is not necessarily filled with roses and sunshine. It takes the right lens— the one with RESILIENCE—to see the day in a certain light. The more present we are to letting go and letting our lives change as well as the people in them, the happier and more joyful we will become. The more we hold on tight to things that need to be released, the more stagnant and unhappy we become and the less joyful we'll feel.

Release. Renew your commitment to living the life you imagine every day. Be resilient—not because you have to, but because it is who you will allow yourself to become through your words, actions, deeds, and experiences.

Here's to blue skies and rose-colored clouds! I hope you'll join me up here where the ospreys soar with happiness and joy!

Jennifer S. Wilkov's passion for communication has led to her being a media personality and producer, a #1 international bestselling author, an international speaker, an award-winning freelance writer, a successful book business consultant, and an entrepreneurial mentor. She knows what it takes to live the life you love in the face of any challenge. Using simple techniques and engaging exercises, Jennifer loves to inspire people everywhere with the insights, knowledge, and wisdom to live the lives they imagine.

www.jenniferswilkov.com

FINDING MY VOICE

Benita Williams

When I was around seven years old, I was playing on the swings at my school. A bunch of kids were jumping out of the swings because that was the cool thing to do at the time—to see who could jump the highest and furthest. I decided to give it a try. I remember another kid pushing me in the swing so I could gain momentum and go as high as I possibly could before the jump. All of the kids were shouting the count: one, two, three!

On the count of three, I jumped out of the swing that was soaring high in the air. The only problem was that as I was jumping out, the seat of the swing quickly pulled me back; instead of launching forward, I found myself falling backward. I fell—hard. Mr. Allen, the classroom assistant, quickly picked me up and carried me back to my classroom. I had a bloody nose, an excruciating headache, a busted lip, and scars on my face. The school contacted my mom, and she took me to the hospital, where I discovered that I had hearing loss in both ears. The next six months consisted of constant migraines, doctor visits, and adjusting to life with a hearing impairment.

Little did I know then that this incident would connect me to a greater purpose: self-advocacy.

I accepted a position at a nonprofit disability rights organization during my college years. I would spend the next twenty-one years at this organization learning about disability rights, self-advocacy, and grassroots organizing to affect change within local, state, and government entities. I developed the skill set to listen attentively to the needs and desires of others and to lend my voice to those who otherwise would not have a voice to speak their truth. I learned how to effectively communicate with others so I would not misunderstand or misrepresent what mattered the most to this population. I excelled to the highest level within the organization, and I was highly regarded by my colleagues.

At the same time, I met and married the love of my life, who happened to have a physical disability. I discovered that being a caregiver required much of the same skill set I had developed as an advocate: being attentive to the needs and desire of others, communicating effectively, and having the ability to figure things out "grassroots" as I went along.

Advocating for others, much like caregiving, is helping them experience life on their own terms. I wholeheartedly believe that people deserve to have an equal opportunity to live the quality of life they desire. While I believed this for others, I did not believe this for myself. Sometimes the advocate is the one who needs advocacy; the caregiver is the one who needs care.

In 2012, I lost a total of twelve people in my life, including my spiritual father and my dear mother. My mom, whom I absolutely loved, respected, and admired, had cancer. I became her caregiver for a period of time; it was a role I was very familiar with and would gladly do again. When my mom passed away, I did not realize how her death would impact me until almost a year and a half later.

On June 14, 2014, I was scheduled to go on a business retreat when my boss noticed I was having signs that mimicked a stroke. Although I did not "feel" I was having a stroke, my face was disfigured, and I knew something was terribly wrong. I went to the doctor, and after checking all of my vitals, I learned that I was having a neurological misfiring of nerve cells that caused facial spasms—most likely due to extreme fatigue, burnout, overwhelm, and exhaustion. At this moment I realized the weight of everything I was carrying. The doctor scheduled two MRIs, a host of medical visits, and some prescription medications. I was unable to go back to work or operate a vehicle. A home health agency provided additional assistance and caregiver relief while I focused on getting "me" back. In the midst of lending my voice and myself to others, I had forgotten how to advocate (speak up) for myself or provide my own self-care.

What I learned during my period of self-healing is that self-care is essential to peak performance. It is important to live your life being kind to yourself. We are taught how to be kind and considerate to others, but we are not taught how to be kind to ourselves. Putting yourself first does not mean that you are neglecting others. It means you are doing what you need to do for yourself so you can show up stronger for others.

I am grateful for the journey; I am more grateful for the grace given to me so that I can be here to help others by sharing my story. Self-care does not mean that you are weak; it means you are smart enough to pay attention to your body and do what you need to do so it does not begin to break down.

I shared the story about my hearing loss in the beginning because I wanted to share the gift in it. The gift is that I've learned how to listen carefully and attentively to my own voice as well as to the voice of others who may feel they don't have a voice or whose voices are not heard. I want you to know that I hear you; I relate to you, and I am here (hear) for you—to champion with you, advocate with you, and help you take action to regiment yourself toward better self-care. Personal optimization leads to the quality of life you truly desire . . . the kind of life where you will swing high—and when you jump, you will soar to new levels!

Benita Williams empowers women to live the life they truly desire. Benita is an award-winning author, speaker, and coach who thrives on personal optimization. She believes the key to success is knowing how to regiment yourself for the success you desire. Benita is married to Coach A.M. Williams, and they reside in North Carolina.

www.benitawilliams.com

I Am Valuable

Mia Williams

What is inside your backpack? What are you carrying around?
What are the ingredients of your heart?
What is deep in your heart? What are you saying?
What have you been speaking? Are you speaking words of life or death?
Where do you see yourself? How do you view yourself?
What is your identity? What defines you?

Several years ago, I started a meet-up for women. For ninety days, we intended to follow a book called *Becoming the Woman I Want to Be: A 90-Day Journey to Renewing Spirit, Soul, & Body* by Donna Partow. Day one of the journey started with thirty-six women. By the last few days, only two women—one other young lady and I—completed the journey.

I saw how easily these women gave up on what they desired. As I watched the women in the group and see other women in my daily life give up so easily, several concerns have been placed in my heart, crucial things that women need to understand before we can pursue being the women we desire to be.

First and foremost, women must learn to know their identity and what defines them. Additionally, we must believe we are valuable. We must learn the power of forgiving and of relinquishing full control of the challenges that come our way. Finally, we must embrace available time for ourselves, find balance, and move forward in our lives.

By putting these words on paper and sharing my perspectives, experiences, and the thoughts that have shown up in my life, I hope to provide you with the guidance you need to help you manifest the life you desire. In this chapter we will discuss your identity, what defines you, and the meaning of being valuable.

Valuable (adjective): 1. having qualities worthy of respect, admiration, or esteem; 2. very important; priceless. A valuable person is admired, appreciated, beneficial, cherished, dear, esteemed, helpful, important, precious, profitable, respected, treasured, valued, and worthy.

You have to know who you are and believe that you are valuable. You are not a mistake. You are here on this earth for an important purpose. You are not here to allow people to abuse, mistreat, take advantage of you, dictate your purpose in life, or define your identity. You are valuable.

When you see yourself as a valuable person, you will not accept anything less. You will only desire to be respected, honored, and cherished. But first, it has to start with you.

I think about all the foolish relationships I experienced before meeting my husband. It took years for me to realize that I had to know myself deep inside and to understand what my qualities are. One day, I finally got it: I cannot expect anyone to respect, cherish, and honor me if I do not respect, cherish, and honor myself first. But if I do not know what I am made up of, if I do not know my identity, how can I do these things?

Knowing who you are, having confidence, and being free from bondage is the foundation to begin. If you are not free from bondage, you cannot get to know your heart's ingredients. Bondage blurs your vision, like wearing a blindfold throughout the day. Until it is removed, you will be unable to move forward successfully. You must locate the key that unlocks what is holding you back from learning and knowing your identity.

So many of us have allowed incidents in our lives from when we were kids, teens, or young adults to dictate our life and define us. From little girls, teenagers, young ladies, and now women, we have stuffed it all in our backpacks and carried it with us, sometimes not even realizing it.

Abuse, disappointment, hurt feelings, broken hearts, being lied to, or lied about, cheated on, talked down to, betrayed, raped, molested, bullied . . . the list goes on. These things are often done by someone near to our hearts—a parent, grandparent, best friend, boss, sibling, child, significant other, or spouse. Some of us have been abandoned or feel we have been abandoned. It is all painful—but whatever it was for you, it does not define you. No matter what it was, you are not by yourself and it's not who you are.

As women, we must be prepared to face many obstacles, learn how to cope in a healthy way, and use challenges as weapons to make us stronger so that they do not lock us up in a holding cell of misery.

It is important to understand and know who we are and what we are made of because this is what will define us. If we do not know what we are equipped with, when we get hit, we will think we are defeated. Always remember this: What we think, we will speak, and it will manifest.

What thoughts are you allowing to consume you? What are you speaking?

Did you know that there is a greater purpose to your life? Current circumstances, incidents in your past, and what people say about you do not define you.

In life, everyone's pain comes from somewhere, but there is good news. You are beautiful, you are beloved, you are fearfully and wonderfully made, and you are made for excellence and greatness. You are strong, victorious, and a winner. You are valuable. It's up to you to believe it from your heart, speak it, and define your identity.

Examine yourself, watch, stand fast in faith, be brave, be strong. Live in peace, live honestly and be authentic. Do not give up or be discouraged. See the present from the perspective of the future.

When you know your identity, it is easy to speak what defines you. It works together.

Let me end with two more questions: What do you need to shed to get some clarity of purpose in your life? What do you need to put off and put on?

I dare you to say it!

Mia Williams is a coach, consultant, and speaker. She's on a mission to meet people where they're at and walk alongside them on their journey. Her goal is helping people see the path designed specifically for them, believe in who they are, possess what they have inside, and go after their purpose.

www.dareyoutosay.com

It Starts with You

Mary Wong

I'm late. Again. I gather my papers and run out the door to the meeting, plastering a smile on my face to hide my frustration.

"Jenny!" I say warmly. "It's lovely to see you—thank you for your patience. Come in, sit down."

As we enter the office, Jenny is frowning slightly. "I have another meeting after this one, so I have to leave by 10:45 a.m," she says.

Oh God, now I have to rush the session.

"Oh dear, I am so sorry; things have been against me today. I guess we all have those days." I offer a double session next week to make up for today, and we get started. The session doesn't go so well—she and I are both under pressure to perform, and our creative juices don't flow.

"It's a good thing we have a double next week. I'm looking forward to achieving more," she says as she leaves.

Not good enough, Mary. Make sure there is a full hour free prior to her next appointment. You are letting your clients down.

Later that evening, as I tuck my youngest into bed, I notice a tear running down his cheek. "Hey, what's wrong?" I ask.

"Nothing."

"Doesn't look like it."

"You can't fix it, so don't worry about it," he mumbles.

"Mate, if something is bad enough to bring a tear, then it's something you need to share. Come on, out with it," I say with an encouraging smile and hug.

"I thought I was allowed to go to Alex's party."

"Yes. Of course you are—why wouldn't you be?"

"It was yesterday. They were all talking about it today at school, and Alex asked me why I didn't come. He said it was rude to say you are coming and to not turn up." His voice was small and full of pain.

I gasp. "No! I thought it was next weekend!"

Oh my God! I'm a terrible mother! I've let my child down.

I spend the next half hour comforting him, before he finally drifts off to sleep. Defeated, I head to the computer to continue the work I didn't finish earlier.

God! I need a break! What else will go wrong today? That's when the email pops up on my screen. WHAT DID YOU DO FOR YOU TODAY? it asks.

Hah! As if I have time to do something for me! The thought stops me in my tracks. *Wow! I know better! What is it I tell my clients? Fill your own cup or you won't have anything to give to others!*

This kind of moment happens less often now, but there was a time when I wasn't even aware that I was falling into a pattern of over-giving and no self-care. I just felt drained, used up.

It was a pattern modeled perfectly by most of the women who surrounded me in my childhood. I was taught to give constantly, but never to receive. Receiving was the equivalent of greed.

At Sunday school, we were taught that the meaning of joy was to live your life in this order: Jesus, Others, Yourself (JOY). This came with the disclaimer that Jesus looked after others but not himself, despite biblical references to Jesus taking time to be alone, to think, to meditate, to pray.

My primary role model was my mother. Living in the country, not driving, and having six children in eight years meant that she had no time for herself. She regularly got only two or three hours of sleep a night after completing her chores.

She had a tough childhood, where she learned to work very hard simply to exist, and she brought that lesson into our upbringing. We were taught to give, give, give and work, work, work—play had little value.

I remember Mum spending hours cooking special food for supper at Dad's regular Lodge meetings. The meeting attendees loved Mum's cooking (she was a very good cook), and they sometimes brought boxes to take home the leftovers. Sometimes those boxes were filled prior to the supper being served, mostly by women who had no children to look after and plenty of time on their hands but who had contributed little if anything to the supper table.

That left Mum feeling used and disrespected.

Many years later I found myself feeling the same way. With the help of a counselor, I started to examine more closely the patterns I had learned in my childhood, and I came to some big realizations.

As women, many of us learned the patterns of selfless giving as children. In fact, we were taught that this was the only way to live; some of us were taught that we wouldn't get to heaven if we didn't live a completely selfless life.

But what happens is that we become overwhelmed and exhausted with no more to give. That's when we attack ourselves for being a bad mother, for being bad at our job, or for letting people down.

And that serves nobody.

Learning to put my own needs first is an ongoing journey for me. Childhood patterns are hard to break. When I find myself feeling overwhelmed, the things that work for me are meditation, time out, and prayer. Funny, they're the same things Jesus took time out to do. He must have known something!

I also find time for fun and play—this re-energizes me and makes the busy times worthwhile. It also builds relationships, connections, and happy memories with loved ones—letting them know that if they are bothered with something, they can reach out and talk with me about it.

This serves all of us.

Meditation, alone time, prayer, fun, and play. I call these five things my fab five, and I encourage you to find your fab five and remember to integrate them into your life. Doing so brings energy, clarity, and purpose.

If you want to make a difference, you must start by taking care of yourself.

Mary Wong's mission is to assist people with world-changing ideas to fulfill their life missions by speaking out, stepping up, and allowing their brilliance to shine. She does this by helping them discover their confidence; clarify their mission and message; and learn to connect, communicate, and engage a following.

www.optimalcoaching.com.au

THE AWAKENING OF ENOUGHNESS

Kamini Wood

Hostage. This is a word that has taken on new meaning in my own personal self-transformation over the last few years and now in my work with other women and teens.

Hostage, according to *Merriam Webster's Dictionary* means: 1a) a person held by one party in a conflict as a pledge pending the fulfillment of an agreement; b) a person taken by force to secure the taker's demands; 2) one that is involuntarily controlled by an outside influence.

As women, we play many roles: daughter, sister, friend, wife, mother, and others. It is when we attach the concept of "responsible for" to those roles that we may find ourselves, simply put, a **hostage to expectations and hostage to external validation.**

My story is just that. I am the daughter of immigrant parents, someone who wanted to fit in and please. The best way I did this was to define my roles through taking ownership and the responsibility for others' happiness and being OK.

Daughter: As immigrants, my parents worked a lot. They were trying to provide more for their family and, in their own way, prove their worth. As a young child, I subconsciously took on the role of pleaser and fixer. I wanted them to be proud of me. And the best way I could accomplish this was through doing well. By not making waves. By being "a good girl." I told myself: "Don't make mistakes. Don't let them worry about you. They have enough on their minds." I felt a sense of responsibility for their feelings. For their happiness. For their comfort. And in turn, my validations were all external. How did they see me? How did the world see me? Was I a good enough daughter? Was I someone to be proud of? This was the internal dialogue that continued to pave my path in the other various roles I took on.

Sister: As a sister, and a younger one at that, I wanted to be accepted.

Once again, the role I accepted for myself was that of pleaser and fixer. If I saw that my sister was stressed, I felt like it was my duty to make it better. I was there to make sure my older sister was OK. Was I being a good enough sister? The validation was externally based.

Friend: As a friend, I never wanted people to be upset or mad. There I was again … responsible for fixing their problems and to fix it when people were unhappy. I was the fixer. If I was not fixing, I thought I was somehow failing the other person. Validation for my worth all came from an external source.

Wife: As a wife, I wholeheartedly felt it was my duty and obligation to make my husband happy. If something was upsetting, it was my responsibility to fix it. If there was a problem, I was probably responsible for that. It became a cognitive distortion. The more I thought my husband's happiness was my responsibility, the more easily I could distort my ownership of things. The validation of being a good spouse was all external.

Mother: As a mother, the role I absolutely took on was that of fixer. I did not want my children to experience any hurt or pain. When my first child was born, I recall looking into her eyes and telling her I would protect her. This of course, was an extremely naïve way to think. There was no way for me to protect her from the hurt of the world. But there I was once more, being responsible for all her happy feelings and her sad ones. Once more, the validation of being a good parent was external.

Why did I do this?

The truth is I didn't realize I was doing it. However, being an overachiever and a people pleaser, my default was defining myself as the responsible party. However, there is a huge difference between being responsible for another and contributing to their life. And that was the shift that needed to happen.

When I was responsible for other people being OK, happy, or things going perfectly for them, I was actually a hostage to expectations. I was controlled by the outside influence of another. The only way I felt worthy was to base my feelings on how happy others were. Ultimately, however, each person is responsible for their own feelings. The more I tried to fix things for everyone, the more I moved into a place of codependency—and so did those around me. I was dependent upon the external validation, and those around me became codependent on me fixing things for them.

Responsibility versus Contribution

Now that I recognize that in all the roles I play, I don't have to define myself as responsible for anyone else. I don't have to be the fixer. I am in control of my choices and my reactions. I am not the owner of someone else's feelings, thoughts, or reactions.

As a daughter, I now understand that I am not responsible for my parents but can contribute to their lives by offering my love and support. As a sister, I am not responsible for making sure my sister is OK, but rather can contribute through my love and support. As a friend and a wife, I can contribute through love and support, but I cannot take the responsibility of making them happy or solving their problems. And as a parent, instead of projecting my ideals and desires onto my children and fixing all their problems, I now approach parenting from a place of unconditional love.

While I can contribute to others' feelings, whether happy or sad, ultimately it is not my job to own their feelings, thoughts, or reactions. It is not my job to decide what is right and wrong for them. Learning that I am responsible for my choices, just as others are responsible for theirs, opened my heart to self-acceptance. I'm no longer a hostage to the expectation of others and external validation—I've stepped into a place of pure acceptance of my own resilience and enoughness.

> *The lesson I learned involved the idea that I could feel*
> *compassion for people without acting on it.*
> Melody Beattie

Kamini Wood, a mother of five, is an international bestselling author, and a certified life coach for teens and adults. Board certified through the AADP, as founder and CEO of Live Joy Your Way and the AuthenticMe® RiseUp program, she works with high achievers on letting go of stress, overwhelm, and anxiety.

www.itsauthenticme.com

Book Club Conversation Starters

This book, *Voices of the 21st Century*, is a vehicle to inspire you to pursue your passion and make a difference. To support you and your book club members, you may choose to use the following questions to start a discussion about sharing your powerful voice and making a bigger difference.

1. Powerful, passionate women with messages share their stories here. What powerful, passionate woman has been an inspiration in your life and why?

2. Which of the stories brought you to tears? Laughter? Deep thought? What in particular moved you to each of these?

3. What causes and messages are you most passionate about? What experiences in your life led to this passion?

4. What next steps are you inspired to take to make a difference? Would you like to do that in collaboration?

5. If you were to write a story, chapter, or book, what would you write about? What impact would you like it to have on others?

6. Given your passions and the areas you want to impact, what organizations might you become involved with?

7. How will you further your leadership in your family, community, region, etc.?

What is your story?
If you'd like to share it within a collective like this book,
visit **VoicesOfThe21stCentury.com**
to find out how you and/or your group can participate.

The Silver Lining of Cancer

This collection of inspirational stories was created in an effort to positively impact the lives of people who have been diagnosed with cancer, and their families.

Our mission is to deliver *The Silver Lining of Cancer* into the hands of people around the world who need some inspiration, hope…and a guide to look for the silver lining at a scary time in their lives.

**Do you or someone you know want to be a guest
on our new podcast, *Silver Lining Conversations?***

We'd love to share your story.
Please apply here:
http://bit.ly/silverliningintake

If you want to help us with our mission, we invite you to purchase a copy and share it with your family and friends, or purchase one as a gift for someone going through trying times.

We also invite you to purchase and donate books that will be delivered to support centers around the world.
More details can be found on our website at:
https://thesilverliningofcancer.com

*"I alone cannot change the world, but I can
cast a stone across the waters to create many ripples."*
MOTHER TERESA

WOMEN SPEAKERS ASSOCIATION

Are You a Global Business Connector?

Women Speakers Association is excited to announce the launch of our Global Business Connector Program. This program is designed for you to own your own platform, leverage the WSA global brand, elevate your presence and reach, and amplify your marketing to increase your bottom line.

As the #1 platform for getting your message heard, WSA provides a Global Success System for each and every member. As a WSA Global Business Connector, you'll be trained, licensed, and supported to hold live events in your community to share your message and connect WSA members to the tools, resources, and training for growing their business.

This business opportunity has a potential six-figure return on investment! It takes what you're already doing, then accelerates and amplifies your results! You are investing in a complete and proven plug-and-play marketing system.

We Want You!

This is perfect for you if you already have an established business or network and you are looking for ways to expand your reach and revenue potential.

 To learn more visit: wsalive.com

CPSIA information can be obtained
at www.ICGtesting.com
Printed in the USA
LVHW05040429052O
656811LV00005B/247